NEW DIRECTIONS FOR STUDENT SERVICES

Margaret J. Barr, *Texas Christian University*
EDITOR-IN-CHIEF

M. Lee Upcraft, *The Pennsylvania State University*
ASSOCIATE EDITOR

Community Service as Values Education

Cecilia I. Delve
Georgetown University

Suzanné D. Mintz
University of Maryland

Greig M. Stewart
University of Maryland

EDITORS

Number 50, Summer 1990

JOSSEY-BASS INC., PUBLISHERS
San Francisco • Oxford

Community Service as Values Education.
Cecilia I. Delve, Suzanné D. Mintz, Greig M. Stewart, (eds.).
New Directions for Student Services, no. 50.

NEW DIRECTIONS FOR STUDENT SERVICES
Margaret J. Barr, Editor-in-Chief
M. Lee Upcraft, Associate Editor

Microfilm copies of issues and articles are available in 16mm and
35mm, as well as microfiche in 105mm, through University
Microfilms, Inc., 300 North Zeeb Road, Ann Arbor, Michigan 48106.

NEW DIRECTIONS FOR STUDENT SERVICES is part of The Jossey-Bass
Higher Education Series and is published quarterly by Jossey-Bass
Inc., Publishers (publication number USPS 449-070). Second-class
postage paid at San Francisco, California, and at additional mailing
offices. Postmaster: Send address changes to Jossey-Bass Inc.,
Publishers, 350 Sansome Street, San Francisco, California 94104.

EDITORIAL CORRESPONDENCE should be sent to the Editor-in-Chief,
Margaret J. Barr, Sadler Hall, Texas Christian University,
Fort Worth, Texas 76129.

Library of Congress Catalog Card Number LC 85-644751

International Standard Serial Number ISSN 0164-7970

International Standard Book Number ISBN 1-55542-837-1

Cover photograph by Wernher Krutein/PHOTOVAULT, copyright © 1990.
Manufactured in the United States of America. Printed on acid-free paper.

CONTENTS

Editors' Notes

In recent years, there has been a call for a renewed focus on the development of responsible citizenship. Lawmakers, reporters, clergy, and educators appeal for mandatory national service for the young in order to create a "kinder, gentler nation." Whether the perceived lack of civic-mindedness is based on reality or not, the time is right to seriously consider how institutions of higher education can influence students' values and their commitment to a more humane society.

The government sector has proposed a number of creative responses. These include the following (according to *Campus Compact Newsletter*, 1988): President George Bush's Youth Engaged in Service to America program, which encourages young people to work with existing volunteer programs that focus on the less fortunate (Weinraub, 1989); the Coalition for National Service's *National Service: An Action Agenda for the 1990s*, which promotes citizenship and seeks to reduce student indebtedness by providing opportunities for service in the military, in the community, or in natural conservation (Coalition for National Service, 1988); the Fund for the Improvement of Post-Secondary Education's public-service grants, which encourage the development of service-learning programs, with the additional benefit of reducing student indebtedness; and legislation introduced by U.S. senators and congressional representatives from across the nation to encourage public service locally, nationally, and internationally.

The positive and sometimes controversial stances that political representatives have taken on public-service initiatives have heightened the public's awareness of and response to the need for community service. The concept of community service, however, is not foreign to colleges and universities. Land-grant institutions were founded to educate and serve their sponsoring communities (Brubacher and Rudy, 1958; Fenske, 1981). More recently, Campus Compact, a coalition of university presidents, was formed to set policy and encourage the revival of the academy's commitment to public service.

Integral to promoting public service on college and university campuses is the development of policies, the design of programs, and the clarification of values regarding such service. Colleges and universities are accustomed to developing new schemes to serve the campus and community; however, it has been some time since institutions of higher learning have actively assumed the responsibility of incorporating values into the curriculum and co-curriculum.

The promotion of values within institutions of higher education has faced many obstacles. Colleges and universities are reluctant to serve as active participants in the molding of values for fear of negative repercussions. Their preoccupation with policies to avert risk from themselves has come to include not only concern for lawsuits that might result from social functions where alcohol is served, but also concern for possible liabilities associated with advising and counseling students.

In their book *Habits of the Heart*, Bellah, Madsen, Sullivan, Swidler, and Tipton (1985) state:

> One of the major costs of the rise of the research university and its accompanying professionalism and specialization is the impoverishment of the public sphere. As Thomas Haskell put it, the new man of science has to "exchange general citizenship in society for membership in the community of the competent" [p. 299].

Faculty have retreated from incorporating social values into the classroom setting and curriculum because of a concern that education might thereby move from enlightenment to indoctrination. In addition, a tenure system that focuses on publication and research over public service has imposed constraints (Florestano and Hambrick, 1984; Newman, 1985).

Administrators and faculty are not the only constituents of the campus community who pose a challenge; students do as well. Astin's 1988 survey of first-year American college and university students indicated that 73 percent felt that "being very well-off financially" was essential or very important to them. The survey also revealed that while over half of the students, 56 percent, believed that "helping others who are in difficulty" was essential, only 22 percent believed that "participating in a community-action program" was very important (Astin, 1989). Consequently, students, faculty, and staff have benignly colluded in the pursuit of educational and career goals while bypassing serious discourse on and challenge of individual values.

Where are the programs to help students make the connection between believing in helping others and influencing societal change? Where are the programs to enlighten students about their community and the world around them, exposing them to those populations that so desperately need their understanding and attention? How do we justify that many students leave our institutions carrying with them the primary goal of "being very well-off financially"?

While there appears to be resistance to the promotion of values development, we are reminded that no situation is value-free (Adler, 1974). That a faculty member or an administrator does not want to incorporate certain values into his or her work with students is a value in and of itself. Given that values are inherent within any college or university curriculum, the players within the campus community have the opportunity to influence positively the values development of students. Inevitably, appropriate programs and supports will assist students in developing and acting on their values. A primary avenue to reaching this goal is through public- and community-service initiatives.

For some readers, this volume will introduce new terminology in the realm of community service: that of service learning. Service learning is more than experience as a volunteer and is different from structured college and university experiences such as internships or co-ops. The term first surfaced in the 1970s. Educators began, and continue, to grapple with a universal definition of this concept. Building on the work of Sigmon (1979), Stanton (1987) and the Coalition for National Service (1988), service learning is the process of integrating academic instruction with public service. It is a collaborative effort whereby students apply their classroom learning to inform and understand an individual or community being served: In turn, students are informed by the individual or community about their needs, concerns, history, and culture. Reciprocal learning results when the server (the student) is educated and develops a deeper sense of civic responsibility and the served (individual or community) is empowered.

Another outcome of student involvement in service is increased empathy (Astin, 1977; White, 1981); that is, the student shifts from a primary focus on self to an increased focus on others. This movement to a larger world view is an essential component of any personal developmental process (Muuss, 1975). Service learning contributes to the preparation of individuals for responsible and continuing citizenry and provides for the recognition of care as a universal obligation—all essential components of a values education.

The editors of this volume hope to encourage increased involvement by, and provide concrete support for, student-affairs professionals, administrators, and faculty as they begin or continue to participate in public- and community-service initiatives. Integrating a values education into every aspect of the students' academic experience will serve to ensure a more advanced, and, one would hope, lifelong commitment to public service.

In Chapter One, the editors present their own five-phase Service Learning Model, which provides the foundation for the rest of the volume. The reader's attention is drawn to the concept of service as a means of learning for both the student and the client population. Developmental theory is referenced as it relates to the model, and examples are used to illustrate the model in action.

In Chapter Two, Greig M. Stewart outlines David A. Kolb's Experiential Learning Model in which four learning styles are described.

Stewart approaches the model in the context of how it can be used to address diversity of styles when designing and implementing service-learning programs.

Chapter Three focuses on the integration of public service into the curriculum. Jon Wagner argues for the integration of teaching and research into service experiences in order to create opportunities for student reflection and for curricular renewal.

The next three chapters address the integration of public service into the academic support programs on college and university campuses. In Chapter Four, Cecilia I. Delve and Kathleen L. Rice focus on campus activities and on how service is related to leadership. Within the context of campus activities, the authors highlight the concept of the servant leader and the goal of developing responsible citizenry within our student population. In Chapter Five, Ronald A. Slepitza applies the Service Learning Model to programming in residence halls and explains the conditions necessary for residence-hall service-learning programs to flourish. Erin D. Swezey offers a brief overview of the development of faith in Chapter Six and discusses how campus ministries contribute to the development of service-learning programs.

Chapters Seven, Eight, and Nine explore the role of the community in community service and values education, the relationship between the campus and the community-service agency, and the need to integrate principles of good practice into campus-based service programs. The development of this section was greatly assisted by the contributions of Barbara Baker, currently of the National Society for Internships and Experiential Education. Steven K. Schultz focuses on the role of the community in shaping students' values in Chapter Seven. In Chapter Eight, through the basic program model of assessment, design, implementation, and evaluation, Debbie Cotton and Timothy K. Stanton address the need for the campus and community to form a partnership in an effort to effect societal change. And in Chapter Nine, Sharon G. Rubin outlines how five hypothetical colleges and universities apply the Service Learning Model to their campuses. She closes with a discussion of ten principles of good practice for service-learning programs, which were generated at a recent Wingspread retreat sponsored by the Johnson Foundation.

The authors wish to acknowledge their deep appreciation for the support received from the National Society for Internships and Experiential Education (NSIEE) along with the care and contribution of their colleagues, associates, families, and friends.

Cecilia I. Delve
Suzanné D. Mintz
Greig M. Stewart
Editors

References

Adler, P. S. "Beyond Cultural Identity: Reflections on Cultural and Multicultural Man." *Topics in Cultural Learning*, 1974, *2*, 23-40.

Astin, A. W. *Four Critical Years: Effects of College on Beliefs, Attitudes, and Knowledge.* San Francisco: Jossey-Bass, 1977.

Astin, S. "Attitudes and Characteristics of This Year's Freshman." *Chronicle of Higher Education*, January 11, 1989, pp. 33-34.

Bellah, R. N., Madsen, R., Sullivan, W. M., Swidler, A., and Tipton, S. M. *Habits of the Heart.* New York: Harper & Row, 1985.

Brubacher, J. S., and Rudy, W. *Higher Education in Transition.* New York: St. Martin's Press, 1958.

"Campus Compact's National Meeting: Member Presidents Are Challenged to Link Service and Education." *Campus Compact Newsletter*, 1988, *2* (5), 1.

Coalition for National Service. *National Service: An Action Agenda for the 1990s.* Washington, D.C.: National Service Secretariat, 1988.

Fenske, R. H. "Historical Foundations." In U. Delworth and G. Hanson (eds.), *Student Services: A Handbook for the Profession.* San Francisco: Jossey-Bass, 1981.

Florestano, P. S., and Hambrick, R. "Rewarding Faculty Members for Profession-Related Public Service." *Educational Record*, 1984, *65* (1), 18-21.

Muuss, R. E. *Theories of Adolescence.* New York: Random House, 1975.

Newman, F. *Higher Education and the American Resurgence.* Princeton, N.J.: Carnegie Foundation for the Advancement of Teaching, 1985.

Sigmon, R. "Service Learning: Three Principles." *Synergist*, *8* (1), 1979.

Stanton, T. "Service Learning: Groping Toward a Definition." *NSIEE Newsletter*, 1987, *12* (2), 4.

Weinraub, B. "Bush Calls for New Volunteer Effort." *New York Times*, June 23, 1989, p. A6.

White, R. W. "Humanitarian Concern." In A. W. Chickering and Associates (eds.), *The Modern American College: Responding to the New Realities of Diverse Students and a Changing Society.* San Francisco: Jossey-Bass, 1981.

Cecilia I. Delve is director of the Volunteer and Public Service Center at Georgetown University and co-chair of the Service Learning Special Interest Group of the National Society for Internships and Experiential Education. She is president of the Board of Directors for the Calvary Women's Shelter in Washington, D.C.

Suzanné D. Mintz is assistant director of Experiential Learning Programs at the University of Maryland, College Park. She is a volunteer counselor at Planned Parenthood of Metropolitan Washington, D.C.

Greig M. Stewart is assistant dean of the College of Journalism and affiliate assistant professor in the Counseling and Personnel Services Department at the University of Maryland, College Park. He serves as a member of the Volunteer Issues Committee for the Whitman Walker Clinic in Washington, D.C., where he co-facilitates support groups for persons living with AIDS.

A theoretical framework, from which service-learning interventions can develop, enhances students' educational experiences, fosters values development, and encourages responsible citizenship. This chapter presents a developmental model for the delivery of community-service interventions and concrete examples of students involved in service learning.

Promoting Values Development Through Community Service: A Design

Cecilia I. Delve, Suzanné D. Mintz, Greig M. Stewart

Human society has become technologically complex, resulting in heightened global interdependency. However, rather than observing an era of collaboration and cooperation, we have witnessed a rise in individual and societal egocentrism (Newman, 1985). Because global interdependency and such egocentrism are incompatible, the following challenge is before us: to acknowledge the relationships in our world and to dissolve the artificial barriers that support mutual isolation and excessive competition. In the educational sphere, actively involving students in their communities in order to develop in them a better understanding of the needs and realities of the world around them is a fundamental step required to make these changes. In his ground-breaking book *When Dreams and Heroes Died* (1980), Art Levine supports this view, recommending that in order to combat apathy and emphasize civic responsibility, public service has to receive a higher priority in the colleges and universities.

The inevitable and exciting task of introducing students to active citizenship begins with preparing educators. Serious consideration must be given to how educators can initiate programs and respond to students' developmental abilities to enter into public service. Historically, within the student-development profession, educators have grounded their work in theory; Perry, Kohlberg, and Gilligan have provided much of the ethical and moral base for understanding and developing programs and policies to support and challenge college and university students. However, though there have been calls for the integration of theory into practice (Knefelkamp, 1984), more attention needs to be given to the systematic translation of these models into actual program designs. When students return from serving food in a soup kitchen, tutoring an illiterate adult, or spending the night at a shelter for battered women, their experiences are rarely responded to in a structured and challenging manner.

The Service Learning Model was developed in response to the needs of such students with the recognition that involvement in community service is symbiotic with values development.

Overview of Student-Development Theory

As we begin to explore ways in which service-learning programs might develop and expand on our college and university campuses, it is important to review the existing developmental paradigms that offer the requisite theory base. Specific models of student development can assist in intervention design by providing detailed descriptions of students at identifiable developmental stages. These stages, when translated into means of structuring environments, promote the desired qualitative changes outlined in a program's goals. In exploring service learning as an intervention in student development, authors of three values-oriented paradigms are of particular note: William Perry, Lawrence Kohlberg, and Carol Gilligan.

Perry's Cognitive-Developmental Model. Based on interview research with Harvard and Radcliffe students in the 1950s and 1960s, Perry (1970) developed a cognitive-developmental model outlining an individual's intellectual and ethical development through nine stages. These stages, or positions, imply growth from simple dualism (positions 1 and 2), through multiplicity (positions 3 and 4) and relativism (positions 5 and 6), to commitment within a relativistic framework (positions 7 through 9).

More specifically, individuals at positions 1 and 2 support the notion that knowledge is absolute. There is a right answer to every question. Individuals at the next two positions have a multiplistic approach to knowledge. Questions that once had only one right answer now may have many answers. All viewpoints seem valid. Individuals at positions 5 and 6, the relativist stages, assume that knowledge is contextual and that each component of knowledge is a piece that fits into a larger whole. The move from multiplicity to relativism is critical, for it is a move from the cognitive to the ethical realm of development. In the final three stages, individuals have established their identity in a pluralistic world. Their actions and beliefs are integrated, yet the students have an appreciation for the diversity of their surrounding world.

Kohlberg's Moral Development Model. Lawrence Kohlberg (1975) provides a model that outlines three levels of moral development: the preconventional, the conventional, and the postconventional. In the preconventional level there are two stages. The first stage identifies a person's motivation for obeying rules as the avoidance of punishment, a belief in the power of authority, and the search for gratification. The second developmental stage, the instrumental-relativist stage, describes morally correct behavior as that which satisfies one's own needs; consequently, much effort is spent in manipulating others in order to achieve one's goals.

Stage three, the interpersonal-concordance stage, begins the conventional level of moral judgment. An individual's peer group assumes increasing importance. The individual begins to move from a self-centered viewpoint to adopting opinions that please others and result in the approval of the larger group. Stage four, the "law-and-order" stage, takes the conventional level of moral judgment a step further: individuals believe that social order should be maintained at any price.

Stages five and six outline the postconventional level of moral judgment. While individuals in stage four perceive law and order as paramount in importance, those in stage five understand that laws may be unfair or unjust and may need to be changed through appropriate channels. People in stage six assume universal moral judgment. The respect for the dignity of the individual becomes critical and must be defended over and above any existing law. Civil disobedience may result from adopting this high level of moral judgment.

Gilligan's Model of the Development of Women's Moral Judgment. Carol Gilligan (1982) looks at moral development as gender specific. While previous theoretical models were developed from a male perspective, they were considered not to be specific to gender. Gilligan studies the difference between male moral development, which is generally seen as rationalistic and individualistic, and female moral development, which is viewed as embedded in relationships. Her theory is a three-level model including two significant transitions between levels. It contributes significantly to the practical application of student-development theory.

Level 1 represents an orientation toward individual survival. At this stage the focus is pragmatic and on the self. A feeling of powerlessness is sensed by the individual and relationships are seen as painful. The transition from level 1 to level 2 is characterized by moving from selfishness to a sense of responsibility to others. During this time, one redefines the meaning of self-interest. Attachment and connection to others becomes important, and there is an increasing ability to see one's limitations and self realistically.

Level 2 represents a morality of goodness as self-sacrifice. At this stage, society's values are adopted, acceptance by others becomes of the utmost importance, and there is a tendency to hold others responsible for the choices they make. Protecting dependent and disenfranchised individuals, avoidance of self-assertion, and fear of abandonment are issues facing the person at this level. The transition from level 2 to level 3 is characterized as moving from goodness to truth. At this point, there is a questioning of the logic of self-sacrifice. Moral actions are no longer based on what other people think but on the realities of intention and consequences.

Finally, level 3 also represents the morality of nonviolence. Here, there is a reconciliation of the diverse concepts of selfishness and responsibility through an understanding of one's self and a redefinition of morality. Nonviolence (not hurting others) is fundamental; caring becomes a universal obligation.

Perry, Kohlberg, and Gilligan contribute significantly to the design of a values intervention for students by providing descriptive models of identifiable degrees of moral and ethical development. Unique to the Perry model is his articulation of the alternatives to moral development: temporizing, escape, and retreat (p. 177). These alternatives to development may occur when there is either an overload or a prolonged lack of challenge within the environment. Kohlberg provides the values practitioner with ways of analyzing an individual's relationship to rules and authority, including both obedience and civil disobedience. Gilligan raises the important issues of gender and transition and provides insight into how these two variables significantly affect an individual's development and thereby necessitate different intervention methods. She also legitimizes the universal concept of caring, a concept that becomes critical as our world continues to become smaller, with fewer resources to share among an increasing population. All three models recognize that individuals approach new experiences at different developmental stages, and they allow for the entrance of individuals at the phase that accurately balances the challenges and supports needed to promote their further development.

Key Issues in Designing Developmental Interventions. Theoretical models provide a general framework from which to develop programs and policies. Identification of the variables that move students along their developmental journeys is critical to their individual growth. To begin, since students are greatly affected by their environment, it is important for student-development specialists to consider the interaction of people with their environment (Walsh, 1975). Lewin's seminal work in this area (1936) provides us with the idea that an individual's behavior (B) is a function (f) of the person (P) and his or her interaction with the environment $B = f \{P \times E\}$. This equation provides student-development specialists with the opportunity to design ways of manipulating variables of the equation in order to yield a learning outcome. Results, however, depend on maintaining the delicate balance between the challenges and supports available in any given student's environment (Sanford, 1966). For qualitative change to occur, there must be a significant challenge to the individual student. That challenge stimulates the student to develop new ways of conceptualizing and responding to environmental cues. Should that challenge prove overwhelming, necessary support systems must be in place to prevent retrenchment, stagnation, or desire for escape. As an individual engages in more complex behavior, development occurs.

Descriptive Variables of the Service Learning Model

The proposed Service Learning Model includes five phases of a student's development that result from the student's engaging in certain kinds of service-learning interventions (see Table 1). Four key variables apply to this model: intervention, commitment, behavior, and balance. Each variable has two descriptive classifications.

Intervention. Reflecting on Lewin's equation of behavior as the function of the individual's interaction with the environment, we can see that it is important for student-development specialists to delineate the nature of the interaction of the student in a community-service program with the client population. Intervention, the first variable of the model, has two classifications: *mode* and *setting*. The mode refers to whether the student engages in a service-learning activity individually or as a member of a group. The setting is characterized by the individual's relationship to the client population. The *indirect* setting describes the intervention where participants are physically distant from the service site and the population being served. The *nondirect* setting involves an individual in the actual environment of the population being served, but not in direct contact with the client population. Finally, the *direct* setting involves face-to-face interaction with the service population either at the service site or in another setting.

Commitment. The second variable of the model, commitment, focuses on the service-learning activity. Classifications of this variable are *frequency* and *duration*. Frequency refers to how often the student engages in the activity. Duration of commitment, however, not only specifies the long-term or short-term nature of the commitment but also indicates where that commitment is found. For example, a student may feel a commitment to a student group, a service activity, or a service site.

Behavior. The student's behavior is the model's third variable. The first classification of this variable is *needs*. Needs refer to the psychogenic motivations students have for engaging in service-learning activities. All behavior occurs in an attempt to meet needs (Murray, 1938). The second classification, *outcomes,* describes possible effects upon completion of the service-learning activities.

Balance. Balance is the Service Learning Model's final variable. It relates to the importance of Sanford's work mentioned earlier and underscores the dynamic nature of the learning experience. For development to occur in a period of equilibrium, tension-inducing stimuli must be intro-

Table 1. Scheme of the Service Learning Model

Developmental Variables	Phase 1 Exploration	Phase 2 Clarification	Phase 3 Realization	Phase 4 Activation	Phase 5 Internalization
Intervention					
Mode	Group	Group	Group Individual	Group Individual	Individual
Setting	Nondirect Indirect	Nondirect Indirect Direct	Indirect Direct	Indirect Direct	Indirect Direct
Commitment					
Frequency	One time	One time to a number of activities or sites	Consistent	Consistent	Consistent
Duration	Short-term	Long-term to group	Long-term to activity, site, or issue	Lifelong to issue	Lifelong to social justice
Behavior					
Needs	Participate in incentive activities	Identify with group camaraderie	Commit to activity, site, or issue	Advocate issue	Promote values
Outcomes	Feeling good, personal satisfaction	Belonging to the group	Understanding activity, site, or issue	Changing lifestyle	Living one's values

Table 1. (*continued*)

Developmental Variables	Phase 1 Exploration	Phase 2 Clarification	Phase 3 Realization	Phase 4 Activation	Phase 5 Internalization
Balance					
Challenges	Breaking into involvement cycle	Choosing from multiple opportunities Dealing with group dynamics	Confronting diversity Breaking from group	Questioning authority Adjusting to peer reaction	Living consistently with values
Supports	Activities, nonthreatening, structured	Group setting, identification Activities, structured	Personnel service coordinators, supervisor, volunteers	Partners, clients, volunteers	Community Inner peace
Goals for Transition	From individual to group	From group to site, issue, or activity	From group to site, issue, or activity	From activity, site, or issue to community	From community to society

Charity —————————————————————————— Justice

duced. These *challenges* serve as the first classification. In turn, *supports*, the second classification, empower the individual to act on these challenges. The student eventually arrives, slightly changed, at a new state of understanding. Knefelkamp contributes to the further understanding of the challenge and support concepts in her work on developmental instruction (1974). Experience and diversity are the two elements she outlines that contribute to challenge. Two other elements, structure and personalism (personal attention to the needs of the learner), serve as components of support. These elements are key tools for the service-learning practitioner when designing developmental interventions for the student.

The Service Learning Model: A Description of Its Phases

What follows are explanations of the five phases of the model, including descriptions of each variable and classification (see Table 1).

Phase 1: Exploration. One way to understand the exploration phase is as a time for the "bright-eyed and bushy-tailed," eager to explore new opportunities. During this period, new volunteers are excited by the many opportunities they encounter, are generally naive about the problems facing others, and may be looking for an opportunity to "help" or get involved. They have yet to connect psychologically or emotionally with any one group on campus or with any population or issue in the community.

Intervention. The individual either identifies an opportunity to participate at a service site but does not interact with the site population (nondirect) or supports charitable activities on campus (indirect).

Commitment. The involvement by students is infrequent; typically, it is limited to one time only (frequency). Consequently, their total service involvement is short-term (duration). The commitment can be to the experience, the group sponsoring the activity, or the issue to which the activity is directed. Generally, that commitment is not a conscious one.

Behavior. The kinds of activities in which the student participates are based on clearly identifiable needs. As examples, a student might be responding to the potential status derived from participation in an activity or a T-shirt to be received after participating or contributing. However, the overlying outcome is the personal satisfaction the student experiences from having participated in the activity.

Balance. The challenges a student faces in phase 1 generally relate to breaking into the involvement cycle. The uncertainty of the activity or the issue being addressed may be of some concern. In order to reach a balance, opportunities to get involved must have structure and must clearly outline what is expected of the student. The nonthreatening nature of the activity serves as a support in this initial phase.

Phase 2: Clarification. During the clarification phase, sometimes perceived as "the salad bar approach," students begin to explore the various opportunities and make critical decisions about where they will exercise their community-service energies. In their attempt to select a specific campus peer group, they also have an opportunity to investigate a variety of volunteer options. Through the diversity they experience with friends and at the placement sites, the students begin to clarify what is important to them.

Intervention. The student participates in a service activity via a group with which he or she is beginning to identify. Service is either nondirect, indirect, or direct.

Commitment. The student engages in a single experience with the group at a number of sites. An example of such activity is a series of service projects required by a fraternity or sorority. A long-term commitment is made to the group.

Behavior. The service activity helps confirm identification with the group. The feeling of camaraderie and belonging reinforces repeated engagement in the group's activities. As a result of the allegiance to the group, the individual is accepted by the group.

Balance. The challenges at this stage involve eliminating options and choosing between service opportunities. Also, students become aware of previously unrealized internal dynamics and possible conflicts within the group. The supports include the security of being with a group, a sense of identity resulting from affiliation with the group, and continued structured activities.

Phase 3: Realization. The realization phase is often a favorite for educators. During this period, the student generally becomes aware of what the service-learning experience is all about. With the exclamation "Aha!," students realize how the seemingly diverse aspects of their community service all fit together. Usually through a profound transforming experience, the student is able to grasp a larger truth for himself or herself; as a result, students become focused on a particular population or issue and more confident in their beliefs. At this phase, the concept of reciprocal learning becomes clearer to the student.

Intervention. The student may continue to volunteer with a group (one that now focuses on a particular service site or activity) or independently. In either instance, the intervention may be direct, indirect, or a combination of the two.

Commitment. The student volunteers consistently and frequently and offers a long-term commitment to the site, the activity, or the issue.

Behavior. The student begins to focus involvement on the particular activity, site, or issue. As a result, students' awareness and understanding of the service site is heightened. Consistency is prompted by their interest in the work they are doing and the excitement that results from its perceived relevance to their lives, whether their life is oriented to their academic or professional career, to religion, or to a form of humanism.

Balance. The challenges involve confronting the diversity of people and environments with which the student interacts. Between the clients, other volunteers, and the staff, the student is exposed to different cultures, subcultures, communication styles, and lifestyles. In addition, the student is often confronted with the politics affecting their service work or within the service agency. The campus volunteer coordinator provides supports through structured reflective activities and individual advising and counseling. On-site supervisors and other volunteers also provide support. The excitement of this stage feeds the individual's involvement. Given that one's excitement at times can override one's ability, the coordinator needs to monitor the student's potential for burnout.

Phase 4: Activation. The activation, or "question authority," phase is an exciting time to witness a student's development from cognitive bystander to full participant in the discussion of the larger and more complex questions of racism, classism, and economic injustice. The student may now feel a strong sense of solidarity for the population with which he or she works and may become an advocate on its behalf. The activist may represent all spectrums of cognitive development, and the public-service coordinator or a faculty member has the challenging task of encouraging students to develop a more complex reasoning ability. Students begin to recognize the reciprocity between serving and learning as they receive more from their service than they are giving.

Intervention. The student is involved directly in the community and/or is intently working on a particular issue in an indirect capacity. Most likely, students will continue their direct contact with the client population. The intervention may be with a group that works together in dealing with a community issue or issues, or independently.

Commitment. The student volunteer consistently offers a lifelong pledge to the issue or issues with which he or she identifies. His or her participation is constant.

Behavior. The student's lifestyle changes to reflect his or her commitment, and the result is a considerable amount of time spent in the community where he or she is serving. It is likely that the student will develop friendships within the served community and with other volunteers. The student advocates issues relevant to the community with which community members identify. The student is motivated by the injustices he or she witnesses. This may result in resistance to and challenge of the college or university representing "the system"; the student may then retreat or temporize in his or her development.

Balance. Challenges are posed by society's response and reaction to the issues raised, by what the student learns in class, and by the concept of the college or university as an intellectual sanctuary where questions about issues of justice are constantly being asked. Because students exhibit their commitments through their appearance, lifestyle, and verbal and written expression, they might be challenged by the reactions of their peers. Their supports are now largely garnered from other students and community members who share similar commitments and concerns. Campus volunteer coordinators assist by offering their time and support and by listening to the problems experienced by the student. This support helps to offset potential burnout, temporizing, or escape.

Phase 5: Internalization. The internalization phase describes those few students who fully integrate their community-service experience into their lives and, as a result, make lifestyle and career decisions consistent with the values gained from such experience. Sometimes envisioned as the "Mother Theresa" or "Ghandi" phase, these students are no longer content with seeing their work in the community only as a function of their school experience. They take steps to make lifestyle choices that incorporate community values.

Intervention. In the final stage of the model, the student is involved in community service both directly and indirectly.

Commitment. Students strive to live a life integrated with their service work; their commitment is consistent, and they pledge a lifetime to the pursuit of social justice in society.

Behavior. The student promotes his or her values in everyday life and consciously integrates those values into his or her being.

Balance. The challenges posed to the student are those that relate to trying to live a consistent lifestyle. Of concern are issues regarding allocation of one's money and resources to effectively reflect one's commitments and choice of a career consistent with one's values. The supports come from the sense of community students derive from their commitment to public service and the sense of inner peace that goes hand in hand with living one's principles.

Phase Profiles, Developmental Parallels, and Goals for Transition

Mentioned earlier was the importance of relating program models to developmental theory. What follows is a journey through the Service Learning Model that outlines sample student profiles, goals for students, and developmental transitions to advanced service-learning phases. Parallels with other developmental paradigms are also described and presented in Table 2.

Table 2. Comparison of Student-Development Theory with the Service Learning Model

Service Learning Model Phases	Perry	Developmental Theorists		
		Kohlberg	Gilligan
Phase 1: Exploration	Dualism Position 1: Authority and absolutes are undifferentiated and therefore unquestioned. Dualism Position 2: Issues are perceived as black and white, right or wrong. No gray. Knowledge is absolute. Right answers are in the authority's domain. Multiplicity is perceived but suspect and opposed.	Preconventional Stage 1: Punishment and Obedience Avoids punishment, achieves gratification. Little sense of moral connectedness. Defers to power. Preconventional Stage 2: Instrumental Relativist Self-centered relationships with others and environment. Manipulation of others in order to obtain rewards.	Level 1: Orientation to Individual Survival Pragmatic focus on self. "Should" and "would" interchangeable. Subject vs. citizen, lack of power sensed. Only responsible to self. Relationships seen as painful.
Phase 2: Clarification	Multiplicity Position 3: Variety of answers. More gray, no wrong opinions. Opens door to learning to distinguish ways of believing and judging. All opinions are valid.	Conventional Stage 3: Interpersonal Concordance Conforming to good boy/nice girl stereotypes—approval seeking. Good behavior is that which pleases others. Conformity to majority opinion. Conventional Stage 4: Law and Order Doing one's duty. Authority is always right. Maintains social order for order's sake. Rules separated from feelings of approval.	Transition 1: Selfishness to Responsibility Redefines self-interest. Attachment; connection to others becomes important transition variable. Ability to see self and limitations realistically. Disparity seen in "would/should." Enhancement of self-worth.

Table 2. *(continued)*

Service Learning Model Phases	Perry	Developmental Theorists		
		Kohlberg	Gilligan	

Service Learning Model Phases	Perry	Kohlberg	Gilligan
Phase 3: Realization	Multiplicity Position 4: Individual begins to see differences between unconsidered belief and a considered judgment. Relativism is perceived.	Postconventional Stage 5: Social Contract "Right"—individual rights, human dignity. Emphasis on set rules reached by consensus. Laws exist to protect these rights.	Level 2: Goodness as Self-Sacrifice Adopts societal values. Acceptance by others paramount. Needs for security. Holds others responsible for the choices he or she makes. Assertion dangerous—immoral in its power to hurt, leads to abandonment. Choosing between dependence and care leads to frozen judgment and activity. Desire to protect the dependent and unequal.
Phase 4: Activation	Relativism Positions 5 and 6: Knowledge is contextual and relative. Almost too much gray. All answers are valid. Resists decision making, closing options. Moving to "6" leads to realization of need to choose. Authorities once again are valued, this time for their expertise, not position.	Postconventional Stage 6: Social Contract (continued) Unjust laws must be changed through consensus and rational deliberation.	Transition 2: Goodness to Truth Questions logic of self-sacrifice. "Selfish" reappears as transition variable. Moral action no longer based on what others think but on realities of intention and consequence.
Phase 5: Internalization	Commitment in Relativism Positions 7–9: Affirms self and responsibilities in a pluralistic world. Has come to terms with self. Established identity. Commitments such as religion, career, partnership in life's experience. No longer "fence sitter." Action is integrated with self.	Postconventional Stage 7: Universal Ethical Rules followed are more subjective and abstract. Concerned with justice, reciprocity, equality, and individualism. Decisions of conscience based on high value of human life, equality, dignity.	Level 3: The Morality of Nonviolence Reconciles diverse concepts of selfishness and responsibility through self-understanding and morality definition. Nonviolence (not hurting) is premiere. Care is a universal obligation. Issues: self-worth in relationship to others, claiming power to choose and assuming its responsibility.

Phase 1: Exploration

Nondirect. Sarah, a student at Wye College, participates in an organized campus program sponsored by a campus group. The organization has assumed the task of painting the local soup kitchen. Sarah does not interact with the target population; rather, she participates in a function that peripherally affects that population. Her motivation is the material gain—a T-shirt, which she receives on completion of the project. She also has gained a sense of personal satisfaction as a result of her actions. Sarah's previous involvement with social issues has been limited.

Indirect. Jim, a student at Zee College, joins his residence-hall-floor members in sponsoring representatives for a dance marathon fundraiser for cancer research. His participation is limited to collecting money and attending the marathon. Jim and most of his floor members are motivated by the potential prestige of being recognized as the first-place team if they raise the most money. The pizza party for the winning team is an additional motivator for Jim and his floor. Their previous involvement with social issues has been limited.

Developmental Paradigm Parallels. *According to Perry.* Sarah and Jim can be defined as dualists. Sarah is comfortable in the soup-kitchen setting. She is there only to paint. She knows how to do the task, and it is clearly defined. Sarah does not have to think about more perplexing issues, such as why a soup kitchen even exists.

Jim is also satisfied with his situation. He does not think about how the money might be used for cancer research; rather, he focuses on how to contribute to making his team number one. Developmentally, although Sarah and Jim are reaching out to others by "getting involved," they find reassurance doing so in a safe, nonthreatening environment amidst a group of peers where the questions are simple and the answers readily available and absolute.

According to Kohlberg. Sarah and Jim can be seen in the preconventional stage. Sarah is painting the soup kitchen because she knows she will receive a T-shirt in return, not because she necessarily feels a commitment to the soup kitchen or to the hungry. Jim fares much the same way as Sarah. He is raising money for cancer research because he knows that he might be in the first-place team. Both Sarah and Jim are instrumental-relativists: They participate in their respective service activities because they know they will get something in return; that is, a material gain or a good feeling.

According to Gilligan. Sarah's orientation is to her own individual survival. She views her participation as an individual way to accomplish something. Her focus is not on how to get to know other people with whom she is painting or to meet the people who will benefit from the painting. Rather, Sarah's participation in the service activity is self-serving. She wants to accomplish a task and ultimately be rewarded.

Goals and Means for Transition. In order for Sarah and Jim to move from the exploration to the clarification phase, their awareness of the various campus community-service groups needs to be heightened, perhaps through an organization fair. Colleges and universities must also ensure that many structured service activities are available, both outside the classroom and integrated into the curriculum, and that personal follow-up contacts are made to students like Sarah and Jim who were previously involved. Increasing the number of opportunities, varying the ways to access opportunities, and encouraging group activities will enhance the possibility that Sarah and Jim will move along their developmental journey.

Phase 2: Clarification

Nondirect. Pete joins the service fraternity, Alpha Phi Omega, and participates in the organization's activities. He is responsible for participating in ten service projects. One in particular involves preparing bulk mailings to raise money for construction of a low-income, senior-citizen housing unit. Pete's previous experience with volunteering is minimal and limited to indirect and group activities.

Indirect. Caroline belongs to a sorority that sponsors testing for sickle-cell anemia. During the drive, these women escort students through the testing process. While their assistance is critical, the activity is a service with an indirect focus. Caroline is motivated by the group's expectation that she actively participate. Her previous experience with volunteering is minimal and limited to indirect or group activities.

Direct. David and Keesha belong to the Recreation Club, which sponsors an annual "Special Olympics" service project. Although officers of the Recreation Club plan and organize the event, David and Keesha's involvement is direct and limited to the actual day of the event. David is a "hugger," that is, a volunteer offering encouragement to participants after each competition, and Keesha is a "timer," that is, a volunteer keeping record of participants' performance in timed events. Their motivation comes from the expectation by the group that they participate. Also, the competition with the other organizations affiliated with the same national event serves as a motivator. The National Special Olympics Committee will give recognition and present a trophy to the campus club that plans and implements the best program. David's and Keesha's previous experience with volunteering is probably minimal and limited to indirect or group activities.

Developmental Paradigm Parallels. According to Perry. Pete, Caroline, David, and Keesha can be seen as viewing their worlds as multiple and diverse. Each of them is in contact with an increasingly varied set of people. They know that social problems exist and that there are many ways of addressing them, whether it is housing for senior citizens, testing for sickle-cell anemia, or providing recreational activities for the developmentally disabled. All four of these individuals realize that there are many ways to address social problems.

According to Kohlberg. The four students are at the conventional level, both at the interpersonal-concordance and law-and-order stages. The "good boy, nice girl" stage is evidenced by their participation in their respective service activities. They are committed to identifying with and seeking approval from the group; consequently, they are less involved in the actual issue targeted by the activity. Their participation is also consistent with Kohlberg's "law-and-order" orientation. Because they must participate in the group's service projects, they do not question the benefits or problems inherent in those projects.

According to Gilligan. Caroline and Keesha are involved in their respective service activities because they are committed to their group's obligations. They feel as though they "should" be involved in their organization's service activities, yet proceed cautiously because they realize their personal limitations. Caroline's and Keesha's association with their respective organizations serves to enhance their feelings of self-worth and sets the stage for embracing a societal value of goodness.

Goals and Means for Transition. For Pete, Caroline, David, and Keesha to develop from the clarification phase to the realization phase, several challenges and supports will be necessary. Both inside and outside the classroom, these students will need to be exposed to more information about the issues related to their service activities. For instance, as Pete takes on the role of organizer for one of the Alpha Phi Omega service activities, he will need to meet with people who work closely with the service issue and discuss their needs and how best to structure the activity. It will be important for him to read about the community with which he will be working. Caroline will also need to feel safe in the knowledge that she has the support of the campus health and counseling centers to discuss some of the issues she is now grappling with as she learns more about the problems associated with persons who have sickle-cell anemia. David and Keesha might walk into the campus-activities office to reserve a meeting room for their Special Olympics committee. In approving the room request, the campus-activities coordinator might take the opportunity to suggest and encourage an educational program prior to the event on the issues and problems connected with the developmentally disabled.

Phase 3: Realization

Indirect. Maria volunteers in a campus organization engaged in research on hunger and spends a consistent number of hours per week (three to five) at the office, interacting with other volunteers, full-time staff, and professionals. Maria is motivated by the research findings and continues her commitment to the eradication of hunger and its related problems. Her previous experience with social-justice issues has largely been indirect.

Direct. Kwon enjoys working with children and chooses to tutor weekly in the afternoons at a local elementary school. Over time, he becomes increasingly interested in and involved with the process of tutoring as well as with the life of the child he assists. The site supervisor provides individual supervision in the form of site orientation, student assignments, and occasional tutoring workshops. Kwon participates in monthly seminar support-sessions for all campus tutors, sponsored by the campus public-service center. Kwon is motivated by his faith, his career interests, and a sense of commitment to the child and to the site.

Developmental Paradigm Parallels. *According to Perry.* Maria and Kwon can be viewed as realizing there is a difference between an unconsidered belief and a considered judgment. Developmentally multiplistic, Maria begins to realize that there are many reasons for hunger and what her responsibilities are. Kwon begins to see that the need for tutors goes beyond the classroom and reaches into the home and community in which the children live.

According to Kohlberg. Having reached the postconventional stage, Maria and Kwon believe in a concept of citizenship that includes a moral obligation to end hunger and educate our youth, respectively.

According to Gilligan. Maria has a need to be involved in a program that protects those who are not treated fairly—in this case, the hungry. It is important for her to be accepted by society, and she sees her involvement in a vital social issue as an answer to her need for acceptance. By creating a supportive environment, the people she works with in the hunger-education organization fulfill her security needs.

Goals and Means for Transition. Critical to the transition from the realization to the activation phase is the need for structured reflection on and clarification by the students of the feelings caused by their experiences and the knowledge they are gaining that relates to the site community. For Maria and Kwon to move from realization to activation, they will need to make a conscious decision to focus on their respective activities and be prepared for the challenges of diversity they will face in the future. Maria needs to be encouraged by the campus volunteer coordinator, the site supervisor, or a professor to take the next step and get involved in a direct-service activity. Kwon, through classes and seminars, may come to see the connection between poor education and economic inequities. Courses on issues of oppression should be offered to reinforce and enhance the students' understanding of the connections between forms of social injustice. The campus public-service coordinator should provide regular debriefing group-support sessions so that Maria, Kwon, and others like them have an opportunity to discuss their experiences and accompanying thoughts. Only then will Maria and Kwon be ready to move on to the next phase.

Phase 4: Activation

Direct and Indirect. Carlos and Sherry work with the Hispanic-refugee population as volunteer legal aides. Carlos is interested in the legal profession as well as in the economically disadvantaged Hispanic community. Sherry is nearly fluent in Spanish and has an interest in issues regarding political refugees and political asylum. Carlos and Sherry have become attached to their volunteer work and frequently socialize with the largely Hispanic staff and volunteer team. In addition to their weekly activities of securing information from their clients and performing legal research, Carlos and Sherry are advocates, not only for their clients, but for the Hispanic population whom they have come to perceive as victims of the inequities associated with their daily lives.

Developmental Paradigm Parallels. *According to Perry.* Sherry and Carlos are in Perry's relativism stage. They recognize that the expertise of the agency supervisors is critical to the positive outcome of their clients' cases. Sherry and Carlos have a difficult time choosing between the many options that seem "politically correct" for overcoming problems they witness in society. Through the challenges of other volunteers and staff members as well as the client population, Sherry and Carlos have come to feel empathy for refugees as a whole, rather than just for their own clients.

According to Kohlberg. Having reached Kohlberg's postconventional stage, Sherry and Carlos are enlightened to the fact that some laws regarding refugee status are unfair; therefore, they feel a responsibility to work toward changing those laws. They accept the moral obligation to change that which is unjust.

According to Gilligan. Sherry's involvement in Hispanic-refugee issues results from her personal acknowledgment of injustices and not from expectations imposed by others. She does not view her participation at the Hispanic-refugee center as self-sacrificing but rather as necessary. While she is committed to her involvement, Sherry toys with the thought that she might be doing this work because of her interest in improving her Spanish. She grapples with issues of selfishness.

Goals and Means for Transition. In order for Sherry and Carlos to move from the activation to the internalization phase, it is critical that their involvement not result in retreating or temporizing. Their participation away from the campus might cause them to view the college or university as the "ivory tower" and to question its value. It is also possible that students will be swallowed up by a particular site or issue and become unable to witness or empathize with related injustices. Therefore, it is important that those individuals with whom Sherry and Carlos now socialize and interact help them understand that the process of change involves many factions, that no one institution is solely to blame, and that many injustices are connected.

Because negative peer reaction against them may be strong, the campus should provide support for students like Carlos and Sherry through workshops, support groups, and individual counseling sessions. Residence-hall floors that focus on community service can also provide Sherry and Carlos with an environment that helps them come to terms with their own anger toward the social system and achieve a more balanced perspective.

With opportunities to engage in advocacy activities, through research and verbal and written exchanges, the goal is for the student to replace individual-community issues with a recognition that injustices are connected and adversely affect the well-being of all. Hence, the student understands the need for a commitment not only to the immediate community but to the overarching society as well.

Phase 5: Internalization

Direct and Indirect. Emma is an older student, with much exposure to communities and their issues. She spent two years in an underdeveloped nation, providing needed technical assistance. She returns to school to pursue a degree in a field that will allow her to help change policy, to work directly with needy populations, or to do both. She is involved with civic and student organizations that promote social justice. Emma is motivated by the integration of social issues into her daily life and has been exposed to a diversity of issues related to community and societal problems.

Developmental Paradigm Parallels. *According to Perry.* Firmly engaged in a commitment to Perry's relativism stage, Emma has established her identity as one of helping others both directly and at the level of social organization. She has learned how to integrate her values through her career, educational, and social pursuits. As a result of her diverse experiences, Emma recognizes the pluralistic nature of the world and understands how she can best play a role to effect positive change.

According to Kohlberg. Having experienced poverty firsthand, Emma has come to terms with established rules that are often subjective and abstract. In her attempt to live according to a universal ethical principle, Emma sees her immediate community as only a microcosm of global society. Emma brings to her career and social choices the filter of conscience, placing a high value on human life, equality, and dignity.

According to Gilligan. Emma can be seen as striving to live out the altruistic components of Gilligan's "morality of nonviolence" by critically reflecting on her experiences in a developing nation and on what she will subsequently do with that experience. Realizing that she also receives both emotional and spiritual benefits from her community service, Emma gains an ability to reconcile diverse concepts of selfishness and responsibility within herself. Through self-understanding and a redefinition of morality, Emma is able to identify her own view of reality and responds accordingly.

Caveats for Consideration

The Service Learning Model provides faculty, student-affairs professionals, and students with a framework to plan service-learning programs. When using the model, however, it is important that the interventionist be aware of some fundamental assumptions and limitations of the model.

Assumptions

Evolutionary. The Service Learning Model is evolutionary in nature; that is, the final phase described (internalization) is not an end to itself. Rather, phases of the cycle are revisited throughout an individual's life, given the situations and events presented and chosen.

Not Age Specific. The interventionist should not rely on age as a factor when determining appropriate strategies for involving students in service-learning activities. Program planning should be based on the student's level of community-service experience and political and social awareness. For example, a freshman who tutored an inner-city child for two years while in high school may require the challenges and supports of the realization phase, while a senior who has never been involved in community service would probably require the preliminary exposure of the exploration phase.

Learning Through Service. The Service Learning Model assumes that learning will be achieved by both the student and the client population. In order to ensure this, direct intervention, educational programming, faculty involvement, and opportunities for reflection by students are necessary. Typically, the concept of reciprocal learning (when the student and the client learn from one another) becomes evident at the realization phase, resulting in student and client empowerment.

From Charity to Justice. In order for empowerment to occur, service-learning programs must move beyond a focus on charity, such as dance-marathon fundraisers and holiday visits to nursing homes. Programs that focus only on charity delay a student's success at empathizing with the service population. Without that empathy, the student will not come to recognize the members of the client population as valued individuals in the larger society, as well as sources for new learning. As a result, the student will miss an opportunity to learn significant lessons from the members of the client community, individual development will be thwarted, empowerment of both the student and the client blocked, and ultimate societal justice forfeited.

Limitations

Research. To date, the Service Learning Model has not been empirically tested to determine its application across cultures. Given the cultural, racial, and ethnic diversity of students, the varying levels of exposure to social and political issues, and the different ways of perceiving ethical and moral questions, it is important that the student-development professional be aware of the potential need to manipulate the critical variables of the Service Learning Model for individual students. Assessment instruments like Rest's (1974) *Defining Issues Test,* which assesses the application of Kohlberg's paradigm, need to be designed and used by the student-affairs practitioner to monitor student movement along various developmental dimensions over time. These data can be used to clarify the benefit of planned interventions and validate the Service Learning Model.

Conclusion

Today's colleges and universities affect a significant percentage of our population. They can provide environmental challenges and supports that have the potential to encourage responsible citizenry and community leadership, resulting in a more equitable society. Through college- and university-supported service-learning opportunities, students will develop a better understanding of and care for their fellow human beings and thereby become more accepting of our global interdependency.

The Service Learning Model offers a foundation from which to develop service-learning programs. While theories, paradigms, and conclusions are vulnerable in that there are exceptions to every rule, the Service Learning Model has been utilized with success by a number of colleges and universities. Institutions of higher education that have embraced the model as a means for furthering their service-learning programs include Stanford University, Georgetown University, the University of Maryland, College Park, and Creighton University. Although anecdotal data strongly support the Service Learning Model, a tremendous need remains for empirical research. Toward that end, preliminary research findings seem to echo the phases of the Service Learning Model (Schmidt-Posner, 1989).

With strong data supporting the Service Learning Model, it is likely that more institutions will consider service-learning programs as a viable means for values development. Consequently, we challenge researchers and practitioners to join forces in the exploration and implementation of the Service Learning Model. We hope the results will promote more responsible citizenry and advance a path toward a more just society.

References

Gilligan, C. *In a Different Voice.* Cambridge, Mass.: Harvard University Press, 1982.

Knefelkamp, L. "Developmental Instruction: Fostering Intellectual and Personal Growth in College Students." Unpublished doctoral dissertation, University of Minnesota, 1974.

Knefelkamp, L. "The Practice-to-Theory-to-Practice Model." Companion to P-T-P videotape. Alexandria, Va.: American College Personnel Association, 1984.

Kohlberg, L. "The Cognitive-Developmental Approach to Moral Education." *Phi Delta Kappan,* 1975, *56,* 670–677.

Levine, A. *When Dreams and Heroes Died.* San Francisco: Jossey-Bass, 1980.

Lewin, K. *Principles of Topological Psychology.* New York: McGraw-Hill, 1936.

Murray, H. A. *Explorations in Personality.* New York: Oxford University Press, 1938.

Newman, F. *Higher Education and the American Resurgence.* Princeton, N.J.: Carnegie Foundation for the Advancement of Teaching, 1985.

Perry, W., Jr. *Forms of Intellectual and Ethical Development in the College Years: A Scheme.* New York: Holt, Rinehart & Winston, 1970.

Rest, J. R. *Manual for the Defining Issues Test.* Minneapolis: Moral Research Projects, University of Minnesota, 1974.

Sanford, N. *Self and Society.* New York: Atherton Press, 1966.

Schmidt-Posner, J. "The Student Experience of Public Service." Paper presented at the "Public Services Is Here: Where Is the Research?" symposium, American Educational Research Association annual conference, San Francisco, March 28, 1989.

Walsh, B. "Some Theories of Person/Environment Interaction." *Journal of College Student Personnel,* 1975, *16,* 107–114.

Cecilia I. Delve is director of the Volunteer and Public Service Center at Georgetown University and co-chair of the Service Learning Special Interest Group of the National Society for Internships and Experiential Education. She is president of the board of directors for the Calvary Women's Shelter in Washington, D.C.

Suzanné D. Mintz is assistant director of Experiential Learning Programs at the University of Maryland, College Park. She is a volunteer counselor at Planned Parenthood of Metropolitan Washington, D.C.

Greig M. Stewart is assistant dean of the College of Journalism and affiliate assistant professor in the Counseling and Personnel Services Department at the University of Maryland, College Park. He serves as a member of the Volunteer Issues Committee for the Whitman Walker Clinic in Washington, D.C., where he co-facilitates support groups for persons living with AIDS.

*Understanding Kolb's learning theory and applying it to the
Service Learning Model outlined in Chapter One provide
student-development professionals with additional means
to promote the development of individual students.*

Learning Styles as a Filter for Developing Service-Learning Interventions

Greig M. Stewart

Chapter One outlined a five-phase developmental model of service
learning, phases which include exploration, clarification, realization,
activation, and internalization. The developmental goals for each phase,
which promote complexity of intellectual and ethical thinking, were
designed after studying the works of Perry, Kohlberg, and Gilligan.
Whereas those authors provide descriptions of specific developmental
goals, Kolb's Experiential Learning Model offers clues for developing
specific learning abilities through the design of interventions that tap
into individual style preferences and abilities. Since all of us learn differ-
ently, not all students will approach service-learning opportunities in the
same way. Building a program for the delivery of service learning through
a learning-styles filter addresses the rich diversity among learners.

Learning Through Experience

The term experiential learning conjurs up images of outside-the-academy
undertakings such as internships, cooperative education, and field-work
opportunities. Inside-the-academy undertakings considered to be experiential learning include laboratory work, gaming, simulation, and role-
playing. The acceptance of these learning strategies owes much to the
work of John Dewey (1938). At the time, his support for learning
grounded in experience challenged traditional, rationalist, scientific, and
technological approaches to education. Similar to Dewey, Kurt Lewin

(1951) expressed support for the individual learner as an active agent in the learning process through his or her interaction with the surrounding environment. A third theoretician to whom supporters of experiential learning are indebted is Jean Piaget (1952). Coming from within a rationalist school of thought, Piaget conceptualized learning as a process where intelligence is shaped by experience over time. His work met many of the traditional challenges opposed to experiential learning and provided a developmental framework through which we can better understand intellectual growth.

The Experiential Learning Model

The works of Dewey, Lewin, and Piaget provide the foundation for the more recent contribution of David A. Kolb (1984). Looking for ways to foster an individual's ability to best "adapt to and master the changing demands of his job or career, i.e., by his ability to learn" (Kolb, Rubin, and McIntyre, 1974, p. 27), Kolb set out to develop the Experiential Learning Model. Experience is the cornerstone of this model, and like Piaget, learning is viewed as a process. Kolb's model outlines the learning experience as a constantly revisited four-step cycle. This model is value-free in that none of the resulting styles formed from the interaction of the four steps is considered inherently better than another.

When viewed in its theoretical sequence, the model's four steps, or the abilities attained by the learner, begin with *concrete experience,* followed by *reflective observation, abstract conceptualization,* and *active experimentation.* Initiated by an individual's concrete experience, the process moves through a period of reflection on that experience. That reflection stimulates the learner to organize observations about the experience and create concepts around that organization to better understand his or her world. Through that new understanding, individuals find the confidence to experiment actively and thereby enhance their learning. That experimentation leads the individual to revisit the four steps of the cycle beginning with new sets of concrete experiences.

Styles of Learning

Kolb's four steps or sets of learning abilities (concrete experience, reflective observation, abstract conceptualization and active experimentation) interact to form four learning styles. These four learning styles are arranged graphically in a quadrant to form a "learning wheel," for easier understanding. Initially, all learning begins with a concrete experience; therefore it is best to begin exploring those styles where a preliminary concrete experience interacts with the subsequent reflective observation on that experience.

Diverger. In the first quadrant lies the *diverger* style. The learning strengths of divergers lie in their imaginative abilities; they exhibit ease in brainstorming and generating ideas and alternatives. As a result, they are able to view issues and problems from a variety of perspectives. With a strong interest in people, divergers are sensitive to individuals' feelings. They greatly value others and have a keen ability to appreciate the needs and concerns of others. Divergers can often be found in the arts or service fields. Their potential for empathy makes divergers excellent candidates for counseling and advising positions.

Assimilator. Next on the learning wheel lies the *assimilator* learning style. In this quadrant, reflective observation and abstract conceptualization interplay. Prone to inductive reasoning, assimilators are more interested in the logic of ideas and theory rather than practical applications to specific problems. This style is associated with intellectual competencies. Assimilators' interests are more attuned to ideas than to people, and assimilators are drawn to information and science positions. Within the students-affairs profession, assimilators serve well as researchers and theoreticians.

Converger. Like assimilators, convergers have the ability to conceptualize in abstract ways but at the same time combine that with an ease in active experimentation. Convergers apply their ideas in a practical manner, are highly organized, and tend toward deductive reasoning: Their strengths lie in the ability to evaluate, make decisions, and apply ideas. Being good at making decisions, convergers are often found in technological or specialist occupations. Within student affairs, convergers serve as excellent directors of service and program operations.

Accommodator. Sharing strengths in learning from concrete experience and through active experimentation, accommodators are risk takers. They best learn from "hands-on" experience and gravitate to situations where they must adapt to changing and immediate circumstances. Accommodators focus on people and action. Though they are found to excel in the marketing and sales fields, accommodators also serve well in crisis-intervention and front-line service positions.

Important Components of the Model

Structure. Kolb's four steps or learning abilities are arranged conceptually to form horizontal and vertical axes. At the top of the vertical axis lies concrete experience, with abstract conceptualization at its base pole. This vertical axis reflects the Piagetian (1970) view of individual cognitive development as a journey from a concrete to a more abstract view of the world. Likewise, the horizontal axis reflects Piaget's idea that an individual moves from an active (left end) to a more reflective view of knowing (right end). By intersecting these two axes, four quadrants are created. Kolb's Experiential Learning Model identifies each quadrant as a learning style, with each style reflecting a propensity for the two learning abilities bordering each quadrant.

Sequence. The theoretical movement that Kolb describes is not linear but circular. His placement of styles around a circle or learning wheel is intentional. In theory, Kolb asserts that experiential learning is most effective when practiced in sequence. Initial concrete experience once reflected upon leads to the formulation of new concepts. These ideas stimulate active experimentation, which results from the individual's newly perceived choices. The resulting consequences of the choices made, move the learner in a spiral motion to a new level of learning experiences. Not to complete the cycle implies theoretically the thwarting of the learning process, resulting in *partial* learning.

Style Preference. The elements of an experience stimulate an individual's choice of a learning style. We gravitate toward the style with which we are most familiar. As a result of learning abilities shared with adjacent styles, an individual can also pursue styles contiguous to his or her preferred style. As an example, accommodators share concrete-experience learning abilities with divergers and active-experimentation learning abilities with convergers; consequently, those two styles, though not dominant for the accommodator, have aspects that make them accessible to him or her. A person's least-preferred or least-accessible style is the one diametric to the most preferred style because the two share no common learning abilities. The least-preferred style (in the case of the accommodator, that of the assimilator) is *still* accessible but is the least functional of the four styles. It requires more effort on the part of the learner to pursue. Though individuals have a propensity for a certain style, we develop abilities and skills in all styles. Over time, our varied experiences give each of us exercise in all the styles of the learning wheel. The results of the *Learning Styles Inventory (LSI)*, an instrument designed to measure a person's learning abilities (Kolb, 1985), provides a profile reflecting a dominant, two preferred, and a least-preferred learning style.

Spiral Progression. As mentioned, Kolb suggests, conceptually, an upward spiral movement of learning resulting from recycling through the learning wheel. Learning builds on past experiences and contributes over time to the development of a more mature learner. Learning involves not only experience, but reflection, experimentation, and abstraction. Though articulated as a process model, by repeatedly going through this cycle, individuals expand their abilities and build on their experiences. They move toward becoming *integrated learners*, which is the goal of Kolb's Experiential Learning Model.

Stages of Maturation. The spiral journey toward integrative learning is a process through three stages of maturation.

Acquisition. The first stage focuses on the acquisition of basic learning abilities and cognitive structures. What marks the termination of this stage is the recognition by the learner of his or her distinction as an individual from the surrounding environment. This usually occurs at the end of adolescence.

Specialization. The second stage focuses on the acquisition of skills and abilities that allow the individual to adapt to the demands of life tasks such as socialization and pursuit of a career. Adaptive competencies are mastered to meet these demands as well as the perceived expectations of society. The end of this stage is marked by the individual becoming aware of his or her own importance in the world, thereby choosing to fulfill personal needs that may conflict with the perceived expectations of society. Responding to society's demands may not necessarily contribute to personal fulfillment. Indeed, if a confrontation between society and self occurs, the individual can then move into the final maturation stage.

Integration. Up to this point, learning maturation can be viewed as the random accumulation of cognitive skills and abilities that contribute to the well-being of the learner. In the integration phase, the self is no longer seen as a chance collection of abilities and possessions: Life is now perceived as a process or journey with each new experience having purpose. To assist in that process, learning abilities that may have previously been held in check are now more readily accessible to the learner and contribute to the facilitation of that learner's journey.

Individualizing Service Learning Through an Understanding of Learning Styles

For those working directly with students, using a learning-styles filter to implement service learning on college campuses provides student-development specialists with information on how to structure specific interventions for different styles of learners. As an example, accommodators and divergers, due to a focus on people and activity are, in theory, more prone to engage in direct (as opposed to indirect or nondirect) types of service-learning opportunities. In contrast, assimilators and convergers would be more at ease with indirect and nondirect service-learning opportunities. Consequently, the *Learning Styles Inventory* can be an important tool for the service-learning coordinator when designing specific interventions for individual learners. By analyzing the results, a coordinator can personalize particular interventions to facilitate an individual student's development. For example, less-developed accommodative learners may need more guidance through deliberate, reflective experiences. Such reflective experiences are essential components of all service learning. The realization phase of the Service Learning Model is a time for the individual to begin to recognize that the problems of the community in which he or she serves are not isolated ones and that social, political, and cultural webs connect one community issue with another. It is in this phase that campus service-learning interventionists spend extra effort in creating opportunities for reflective experience for students, such as journals, discussion groups, or term papers associated with an appropriate class. Due to their strengths in reflective learning, students with diverger or assimilator skills respond more readily to such tasks than do convergers or accommodators, for whom reflection proves more challenging. Attention to the details of learning styles' by the faculty member or service-learning coordinator can prevent thwarted or partial learning. The circular learning process itself enhances the opportunities for the student to move into more mature, integrative learning.

This situation at the micro level highlights for the student-development specialist the importance of carefully planned interventions. It is at the micro level that knowledge of learning styles can assist in the application of the Service Learning Model. Ultimately, by working with the four different learning styles within the five service-learning phases, the specialist will develop a three-dimensional grid outlining profiles, intervention strategies, and goals for each style in each phase. It is important for the service-learning coordinator to understand that what may prove a challenging intervention for one student may prove less of a challenge for another, given learning-style preferences. It is at these points that the coordinator needs to be acutely aware of the creative tension between challenge and support (Sanford, 1966) and to know when to provide what in the effort to promote the student's overall development.

Parallels of Learning Abilities
and Service-Learning Phases

To promote the development of integrative learning, Kolb argues that partial learning must be avoided. Partial learning results from learners not moving systematically around the learning wheel with each experience; as a result, skills and abilities within each style of learning are not fully developed. The design of the Service-Learning Model supports Kolb's sequencing notion (see Figure 1). How the two models parallel each other is outlined below. Each service-learning phase is presented, and related learning wheel components are highlighted.

Exploration. This phase reflects a student's initial concrete experiences in the realm of service learning. Here the student engages in immediate experiences. Because community service is a new experience and in an unknown context, it is a very personal, self-centered one, generating previously untapped feelings and intuitions about an individual's environment. As an example, consider a new student who during freshman orientation opts to participate in a group service-learning activity com-

Figure 1. Comparison of the Experiential Learning Cycle*
with the Service Learning Model

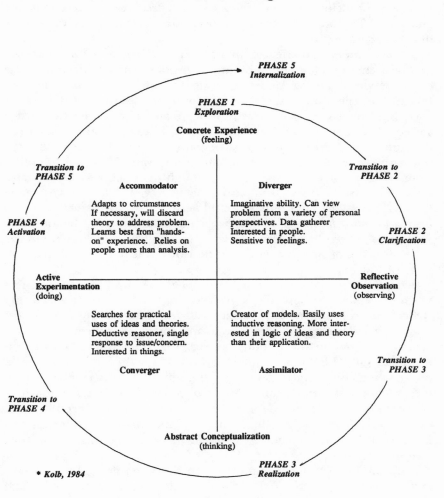

PHASE 5
Internalization

PHASE 1
Exploration

Concrete Experience
(feeling)

Transition to
PHASE 5

Transition to
PHASE 2

Accommodator

Diverger

Adapts to circumstances
If necessary, will discard
theory to address problem.
Learns best from "hands-
on" experience. Relies on
people more than analysis.

Imaginative ability. Can view
problem from a variety of personal
perspectives. Data gatherer
Interested in people.
Sensitive to feelings.

PHASE 4
Activation

PHASE 2
Clarification

**Active
Experimentation**
(doing)

**Reflective
Observation**
(observing)

Searches for practical
uses of ideas and theories.
Deductive reasoner, single
response to issue/concern.
Interested in things.

Creator of models. Easily uses
inductive reasoning. More interested in logic of ideas and theory
than their application.

Converger

Assimilator

Transition to
PHASE 3

Transition to
PHASE 4

Abstract Conceptualization
(thinking)

* Kolb, 1984

PHASE 3
Realization

prised of a day-long painting project at a local Hispanic community center. This student is exposed to other new students and to a unique environment. Before that experience can be *reflected on,* it needs to be *felt* and *sensed.* Exploration is the service-learning phase in which these types of experiences occur.

Clarification. Experiences amass, and there comes a time to *reflect* on this accumulation of thoughts and intuitions. The clarification phase of the Service Learning Model serves as that opportunity for reflection, that is, for generating and sorting out intuitive meanings of the experience. Students come to the clarification phase after having explored a variety of community-service opportunities. The exploration may occur through active service, through participating in activity fairs where representatives of various service organizations are available to explain opportunities for involvement, as well as through discussion with other students. As the student begins to participate in service in a more systematic manner, the student not only *feels* and *senses* these experiences, but also begins to *intuit meaning.* Through placing an increased value on other volunteers as well as on service clients, the student begins to *appreciate different points of view,* a major characteristic of the reflective-observation stage of learning.

Realization. Considered the "Aha!" phase, realization is the moment when the student becomes the active agent in his or her service learning. Reflection no longer remains in the realm of intuition but *involves the use of logic.* The student spends time and energy on systematically collecting information and forming a conceptual framework. As an example, a student who volunteers once a week at a soup kitchen also has a paper to write for a nutrition class. Through the research conducted for the paper, the student becomes aware of some of the interrelationships between government policy, societal trends, and the existing condition of the hungry. *Research* and the ability to *draw interconnections* are the kinds of behaviors endemic to those at the learning stage of abstract conceptualization.

Activation. No longer comfortable in a service role confined by peer and academic structures and norms, a student in the activation phase takes a more self-directed service role. This active focus results from strategies generated through the student's thoughts on his or her feelings and intuitions regarding a particular set of experiences, together with ideas about and analyses of a particular problem, service site, or issue. To continue with our example from the realization phase, the student's move into activation is signaled by, for example, his or her efforts to establish a hunger-action program on campus. Through negotiations with the student government, the dean of students, and the academic vice president, the student succeeds in getting the campus to dedicate a semester to the theme of hunger. Food drives are conducted, speakers and symposia are presented, faculty are encouraged to weave the theme of hunger into their curricula (be it in economics, government, literature, or other disciplines), and the student government engages in external lobbying efforts for better food services within the local community. The example student thus exemplifies learning through active experimentation, by influencing people and changing situations *through practical application* of what he or she has learned and experienced.

Internalization. The final service-learning phase, internalization, finds the student at a different, more mature level of learning. He or she is *open to new intuitions and feelings,* ways of thinking, and taking action. The student's subsequent experience will benefit from the integration of past learning experiences, and as fresh experiences are undertaken, the student will pursue the various learning styles, but at a more mature level.

These parallels between learning-abilities and service-learning phases highlight how systematic movement through the phases of the Service Learning Model assist in the development of a more integrated learner. Though a student may have a preferred style of learning, by deliberately and carefully moving through each phase, he or she is provided the opportunity to build skills and abilities characteristic of each style of learning.

Enhancing the Development of Values

Influenced by members of the school of radical educators, particularly Paolo Freire (1973, 1974), Kolb asserts that the Experiential Learning Model promotes not only the development of individual learners, but also that of a culture. With this assertion, the Service Learning and Experiential Learning models work together in their contribution toward the development of values. By engaging in deliberate and planned service-learning interventions, particularly those designed through a learning-styles filter, students are challenged to clarify and act on their values.

Recognizing the obvious tension between abilities (that is, between feeling and thinking and between observing and acting), Kolb reconsiders the learning wheel in the light of a reinterpretation of its structure (see Figure 2). Kolb describes the vertical axis as a dialectic between value and fact. Value predetermines the concrete experiences we ultimately choose. Fact serves as the foundation for our scientific judgment of these experiences. Kolb clarifies the horizontal pole as a dialectic between relevance and meaning. Where we initially organize our observations to create a meaning from our experiences, we also strive to apply that meaning purposefully through active experimentation.

The Four Virtues of Kolb's Learning Wheel. It is at this point that Kolb introduces the concept of virtue in the process of learning. He

Figure 2. The Values Within Kolb's Learning Wheel

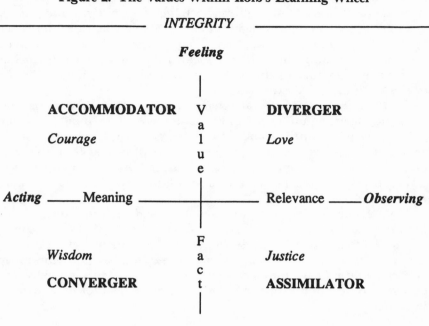

highlights four virtues: love, justice, wisdom, and courage. Each builds on another and relates to a particular learning style or set of learning abilities. All four are governed by the master virtue of integrity.

Love. The virtue of love helps usher divergers beyond their self-centered observations and a personal filter of reflection into a dimension of feeling; that is, to a respect for others. Love catalyzes the learner's ability to empathize with others' feelings and conditions. The resulting empathy challenges the learner to reflect on his or her own experience and create new meaning.

Justice. The next virtue, that of justice, assists us when we are using the assimilator learning style. Often when we approach an accumulation of facts, we make expedient assumptions. A sense of justice filters the learner's observations and thoughts about accumulated facts such that assumptions drawn by the learner are made relevant through fair and inclusive judgments.

Wisdom. Convergers are caught between the tensions of fact and meaning. The virtue of wisdom assists us when using the converger learning style. Wisdom holds random thinking or accumulation of facts in check by encouraging *meaningful* choices about one's behavior.

Courage. For those found challenged when using the accommodator style of learning, the virtue of courage comes into play. Courage provides an individual with the motivation to find meaning in his or her actions and to continue in the practical application of new knowledge. Courage helps the learner prevail over situations which challenge him or her to abandon planned and intended strategies.

Integrity. The overriding virtue, integrity, monitors the four virtues mentioned by calling us to respond to life's condition in an active and empathic manner. Where it may be easier to choose a less complicated road, integrity encourages us to opt for less-selfish paths, resulting in more creative and productive outcomes that contribute to an allocentric world view.

A Call to Transform the Curriculum. Service-learning goals can move closer to reality if the virtues of each style of learning are bred within each learner. First, students, through their experience in serving others, develop the ability to care. Students cannot develop empathic and more allocentric world views without this ability. Caring, when matched with respect, brings forth the virtue of love. Since care is felt and witnessed for all, love opens learners to an understanding of fairness. Next, behavior motivated by concerns about fairness and empathy has the potential to expand beyond charitable actions and to approach just ones. However, for that behavior to be purposeful, it cannot be random. Therefore the virtue of wisdom provides students with the ability to create meaning out of their choices to act. Finally, courage provides students with the motivation to model and promote their values through steadfast behavior and responsible citizenry within their communities.

To love, to choose fairly and meaningfully—these are courageous acts. The curriculum requires transformation through the integration of the four virtues discussed into active learning components. Without these considerations, true learning can only be partially realized. Ultimately, we must engage our students in the clarification of values so that care becomes the motivation for individual, meaningful behavior, and for change to be deliberate and just.

Conclusion

In Chapter One, several developmentally based goals of the Service Learning Model were outlined. They include increased empathy, responsible citizenry, and action generated from a foundation of justice. The achievement of these goals cannot occur within the traditional academic curriculum. Experience is the key component for these goals to be actualized. It must become an integral part of our students' structural learning process. Through a multidimensional understanding and implementation of Kolb's Experiential Learning Model, service learning is enhanced and serves to promote the holistic development of the student.

References

Dewey, J. *Experience and Education.* New York: Macmillan, 1938.

Freire, P. *Education for Critical Consciousness.* New York: Continuum, 1973.

Freire, P. *Pedagogy of the Oppressed.* New York: Continuum, 1974.

Kolb, D. A. *Experiential Learning: Experience as the Source of Learning and Development.* Englewood Cliffs, N.J.: Prentice-Hall, 1984.

Kolb, D. A. *Learning Styles Inventory.* Boston: McBer, 1985.

Kolb, D. A., Rubin, I. M., and McIntyre, J. M. (eds.). *Organizational Psychology.* Englewood Cliffs, N.J.: Prentice-Hall, 1974.

Lewin, K. *Field Theory in Social Sciences.* New York: Harper & Row, 1951.

Piaget, J. *The Origins of Intelligence in Children.* New York: International University Press, 1952.

Piaget, J. *The Place of the Sciences of Man in the System of Science.* New York: Harper & Row, 1970.

Sanford, N. *Self and Society.* New York: Atherton Press, 1966.

Greig M. Stewart is assistant dean of the College of Journalism and affiliate assistant professor in the Counseling and Personnel Services Department at the University of Maryland, College Park. He serves as a member of the Volunteer Issues Committee for the Whitman Walker Clinic in Washington, D.C., where he co-facilitates support groups for persons living with AIDS.

Service-oriented teaching and research can provide valuable opportunities for both students and faculty to move beyond the academic curriculum and to renew the academic culture of colleges and universities.

Beyond Curricula: Helping Students Construct Knowledge Through Teaching and Research

Jon Wagner

While pursuing his undergraduate studies, Gerald works at a soup kitchen on Tuesday and Thursday evenings, helping dispense food to the homeless and poor in a decaying section of a large city. Kathy spends a few hours away from campus each week as an adviser for a rural 4-H club that is organizing an exhibition of domestic crafts. Stephanie finds herself on most Saturdays in the law library, conducting volunteer legal research for a public-interest law firm. David has a part-time job as a tutor in the campus learning-skills center.

The service activities of these undergraduate students can contribute to their personal and intellectual development in a variety of ways, many of which are examined in other chapters of this volume. But how can we characterize relationships between these service activities and the *undergraduate curriculum?* Is there any relationship at all? If so, is it one in which learning and intellectual development are enriched, deepened, or broadened? Or, are service activities working at cross-purposes with the curriculum, either logistically, by competing for students' time and attention, or intellectually and morally, by moving students farther away from the kinds of analysis and inquiry that the curriculum itself is designed to encourage?

These questions about particular students reflect more general questions about colleges and universities. What different kinds of activities can provide students with opportunities for integrating community service and curricular concerns? In what respects are these "service-learning" activities (see Luce, 1988, for a comprehensive "service-learning" bibliography) consistent with the academic goals of higher education? And what structural contradictions are revealed through efforts to promote these activities within colleges and universities?

In this chapter I would like to examine these questions in terms of an emerging "constructivist" model of the relationship between knowledge and learning. A core tenet of this model is the proposition that "the activity in which knowledge is developed and deployed . . . is an integral part of what is learned" (Brown, Collins, and Duguid, 1989). While this proposition may appear relatively straightforward, it has provocative implications for education and schooling. In general, it suggests that programs designed to encourage individuals to *develop and acquire* knowledge must engage those individuals in activities by which relevant knowledge is actually *constructed*. In particular, it suggests that for students to understand their curricula they must participate in activities similar to those through which curricula are designed and implemented in the first place.

This examination of a constructivist orientation for community service and undergraduate curricula challenges two elements of conventional wisdom. First, while the curriculum is usually viewed as a stimulus and resource for the instruction of students, as portrayed here it is also a product of the distinctive service-learning activities of faculty members. Second, while community service is usually viewed as an orientation toward indigent populations or populations in need, these populations are recognized as only a few of the many "communities" for which students and faculty members can provide valuable services.

These alternative conceptions of the relations between service learning and the curriculum are necessary to clarify *pedagogic* connections between the two, connections grounded in processes of acculturation, interpretation, and collective action. They are also necessary in order to understand how service-learning activities—particularly those of faculty members—both generate and renew forms of disciplined inquiry on which the curriculum is based.

Student Reflection

The concept called upon most frequently to describe connections between service and learning is "reflection." This concept is examined within several other chapters of this volume and is central to theories of both "experiential learning" (Kolb, 1984) and "critical thinking" (Ennis, 1989). And for good reason. Reflection is inclusive of a wide range of thoughtful processes, and thoughtful processing is one of the hallmarks of learning.

When focused on particular concepts, reflection also works well to articulate service with curricula. For example, service activities of the students mentioned above could provide opportunities for examining concepts central to one or more social-science disciplines. A student's understanding of anthropology, sociology, psychology, economics, or political science could be enriched by examining disciplinary conceptions of power, community, exchange, ideology, or perception within the field settings of the service activity (Borzak, 1981).

The students mentioned above could also use their service activities to examine some issues of interest to humanists. Questions about ethics, aesthetics, rhetoric, or the interpretation of discourse and ritual could be examined within each student's field setting. To the extent that these questions also frame curricular issues in philosophy, the visual and performing arts, religious studies, or literature, students specializing in such disciplines could increase their understanding of the curriculum as well as use the curriculum to understand better the service contexts in which they work.

Connecting service activities to curricula in the physical and natural sciences is more problematic, at least in terms of the examples cited above, in part because their canons of scientific practice differ somewhat from those of the social sciences and humanities (D'Andrade, 1986). Nevertheless, we can identify domains of action—nutrition and health, agriculture, domestic and manufacturing technology, or environmental policy—in which the natural sciences themselves are central to understanding or providing services.

These observations suggest that with adequate encouragement for guided reflection, service-learning activities can provide active complements to classroom instruction and help students examine issues of importance to discipline-based models of knowledge (Wagner, 1981). But what specific activities are most useful in encouraging reflection? And which of these are most useful in guiding reflection toward matters in the curriculum? To answer these questions, let me examine briefly the service-learning sources of the curriculum itself.

The Community Contexts of Curriculum Design

Faculty design curricula, and they do so as members of several different, overlapping, and somewhat contrasting communities. One of these communities is the campus itself: the students, administrators, staff and other faculty, and the physical and cultural environment in which the institution's affairs are conducted. Another is the smaller sub-community of a department or program. Yet another—and one of the most meaningful to faculty members themselves (Clark, 1987; Smelser and Content, 1980)—are professional communities and associations identified with particular academic disciplines.

Curricula are the product of negotiations between individual faculty members and these communities, negotiations that involve ongoing compromises between what faculty members know, how they want to spend their time in class, and the affairs of the different academic communities in which they participate. These negotiations represent the overall context of action in which curricula make sense to faculty members.

Faculty members exercise their sense of curricula emerging from such negotiations through the service activities of teaching and research. In teaching, faculty members help students to become engaged with curricula and disciplines and to meet instructional expectations of the campus. In research, they conduct disciplined inquiry and report on it in terms useful to their disciplinary colleagues and communities external to the campus.

For faculty members, the service activities of teaching and research create tangible, ongoing connections between curricula and community life in the multiple communities in which faculty members participate. These communities in turn generate continuing demands for explanation, in response to which faculty members must think critically and imaginatively about curricula and about traditions of inquiry that support or challenge their own conception of knowledge and ideas.

The thoughtfulness that faculty members bring to the curriculum is thus embedded in ongoing exchanges with other people, exchanges that affect their reputation, their livelihood, and their opportunities for sociability and esteem. Borrowing a term from the anthropologist Jean Lave (1988), their thoughtfulness is a manifestation of "cognition in practice." To the extent that the exchanges stimulating such thoughtfulness are guided by institutional policies, faculty reflection about relationships between knowledge of the world, disciplines, and curricula can be viewed as an institutional product.

Teaching and Research as Service Learning

The investment by colleges and universities in faculty thoughtfulness about the curriculum reflects an effort by institutions of higher education to embrace dual traditions of inquiry and service. As Edward Shils (1983) has noted:

> Universities have dual obligations. On the one side, they are responsible
> for the maintenance and advancement of knowledge and on the other
> they are responsible for performing important functions for their socie-
> ties. Emphases on these two obligations vary among universities; some
> universities lean more to the former, others more towards the latter, but
> no university can wholly divest itself of either of these obligations.
> University teachers are similarly under these dual obligations. Teaching

at an advanced level and fundamental research are the most important of the activities through which universities meet both these obligations [p. 73].

In some respects, the service dimensions of the process described by Shils are better understood for teaching than for research. However, faculty members themselves routinely try to frame their research activities so that they are of value to other communities (Wagner, 1987). They do this in part because their work requires them to. Research projects must make sense not only to colleagues in the discipline, but also to departmental and campus colleagues, and, for extramurally funded research, to external communities whose agendas may differ dramatically from those of academic institutions themselves. In just these terms, faculty research activities are designed to serve larger communities.

Some of the communities served by faculty teaching and research may include vulnerable or indigent populations as popularly defined. But many do not. Some communities served may not even be perceived by faculty peers, students, or members of the public as deserving of service. For example, academic research directed toward the needs of the military, domestic or foreign governments, political activists, and business entrepreneurs is a subject of great controversy. However, regardless of the community needs addressed by faculty research, the challenge of communicating about that research to different communities creates powerful incentives for reflection about curricula, disciplines, and knowledge of the world.

Thus, through the structured exchanges they engender with different communities, both teaching and research provide faculty members with powerful service-learning opportunities. These opportunities encourage faculty members to construct knowledge that is new for themselves and for others within campus, inter-campus, and off-campus communities. They also create for faculty members a close connection between personal intellectual development and the institutional mission of their college or university, a context in which "learning and acting are interestingly indistinct, learning being a continuous, life-long process resulting from acting in situations" (Brown, Collins, and Duguid, 1989, p. 33).

In addition to helping faculty members construct new knowledge and articulate their own intellectual development with the mission of their home institutions, service-learning opportunities of teaching and research also define the social contexts in which faculty members experience academic disciplines and curricula as meaningful and worthwhile orientations toward the world of knowledge. Because students usually lack opportunities to participate in teaching and research, it is understandable that such connections and meaning are frequently missing from their undergraduate experience. But it is also unfortunate.

Students Teaching and Conducting Research

As a regular feature of their undergraduate education, students could be expected to teach, to provide instruction to their peers and to younger students in surrounding elementary and secondary schools, and to assist other teachers as tutors, aides, and academic advisers. These teaching activities can also benefit other students and teachers. When tied to a student's own area of academic specialization, they can help the teaching student better understand those disciplines of inquiry and expression on which the curriculum itself rests (Cross, 1986).

Student teaching can take a variety of forms and serve a wide range of communities. For example, at one university, undergraduate students who have completed an introductory anatomy class can enroll in a special discussion section, the purpose of which is to assist them in teaching anatomy concepts in local elementary schools. At another university, undergraduates can enroll in independent study courses focusing on the development of language and literacy while simultaneously serving as language-arts teaching aides in nearby schools.

Other communities served by student teaching can be much closer to home. For example, opportunities exist on many campuses for students to work as tutors at campus learning centers. At some institutions, such opportunities are augmented by opportunities for advanced undergraduates to lead discussion sections for large lecture courses or student-initiated courses. At one university, students can complement enrollment in a core course on Shakespeare with concurrent participation in satellite "production sections," in which they prepare plays—live and on videotape—for presentation and discussion with on- and off-campus audiences.

Still other opportunities for students to "teach" can be provided routinely by asking them to share their understanding of books, concepts, or related laboratory and field experiences with their fellow students. If Gerald, Kathy, Stephanie, and David were enrolled in seminars with other students working in related service projects—as is the case for some programs of sponsored, experiential learning (Stanton and Ali, 1982; Little, 1983; National Society for Internships and Experiential Education, 1986)—we can imagine them "teaching" each other a great deal about the settings in which they work, the issues that frame action in those settings, and the relationship of service activities to related social policies.

Undergraduates could be encouraged also to conduct research of value to others, to examine empirically a range of questions that are important to individuals, institutions, and groups on and off the campus. By increasing students' familiarity with the complexities of the world, service-research activities could broaden the impact of undergraduate education. They could also deepen it by engaging students in research methods and designs, developing technical research skills, and becoming more familiar with the complex relationship between research and practice.

As is the case for faculty research, student-research activities could be oriented toward a variety of different communities, some of whose cultures might contrast markedly with undergraduate culture. For example, at many colleges and universities, students engage in public-interest research in order to generate information of value to citizen or consumer groups. Clinical or case-based research of value to service and reform efforts could also be tied to student participation in a wide variety of direct-service roles. Interdisciplinary programs of service-oriented student research are also well-represented within British and European traditions of "project-oriented" education (Cornwall, Schmithals, and Jaques, 1976), within programs of graduate and professional study, and through some undergraduate service-research centers. An expectation that the student conduct research of value to client communities in the field setting is also a routine feature of some programs that engage students in field internships (Borzak, 1981).

Some student research activities can be oriented toward the campus community itself. For example, questions about undergraduate teaching and learning practices represent a rich area for the conduct of socially valuable student-initiated research. Classroom assignments themselves can be framed to encourage student research that is of value to others, and students can also participate in research projects conducted by faculty members.

Because it challenges students to generate, construct, and communicate knowledge to a number of constituencies (see, for example, Hursh and Borzak, 1979; Borzak and Hursh, 1977), service-oriented student research can generate educational outcomes similar to those generated for faculty members through research of their own. This is not true, however, for the kind of research assignment that undergraduates are typically asked to conduct: an enterprise directed entirely toward preparation of a report to a single faculty member, whose sole interest is in assessing the student's research skills. While these assignments have an honored place in the curriculum, their educational value to students—and their social value in contexts beyond the curriculum—are doubtful.

The Pedagogical Dualism of Higher Education

Colleges and universities are best suited to support, embrace, stimulate, guide, and assess forms of service learning that involve teaching or research. Teaching and research are familiar to faculty members as forms of service learning in which they are already engaged; they are familiar to administrators as forms of activity that merit institutional support; and they represent two of the most strategic and valuable extensions of academic culture to the off-campus world. Also, it is to service-oriented teaching and research that colleges and universities attach their own distinctive standards of excellence.

Why, then, are students so rarely encouraged to teach or to conduct research? A partial answer to this question can be found in the logistical demands of engaging students in activities other than memorization and recitation. But a more complete answer emerges from fundamental contradictions between the theories of learning that colleges and universities apply to faculty members and those they apply to students.

Institutions of higher education expect students to develop and exhibit understanding through activities that are relatively passive, individualized, and defined entirely by the demands of the curriculum itself. The two activities that best exemplify student-based pedagogy are memorization and recitation, what Roland Tharp has called the "recitation script" approach (1989). In contrast, faculty members are expected to develop and exhibit understanding through activities that are extremely active, collective, and situated within the demands of larger institutional and social worlds. The two activities that best exemplify the faculty-centered pedagogy are teaching and research.

Within the terms of this pedagogical dualism, faculty members are asked to construct the curriculum through forms of inquiry and communication that extend well beyond it, whereas students are asked to limit their inquiries and communications to the curriculum itself. Following the line of analysis proposed by Brown, Collins, and Duguid (1989), it appears that faculty undertake "authentic activity" in relation to the same curriculum that students approach through "ersatz activity."

At most institutions, these asymmetries remain relatively intact, despite unfortunate consequences for students, academic disciplines and institutions, and faculty members themselves. By limiting student learning to the curriculum, students remain largely blind to their own intellectual skills. They find it difficult to apply skills developed in one area or level of the curriculum to their work in another, to their participation in nonschool settings, or to the balance of their lives (Resnick, 1987). Nor do students develop much understanding and appreciation of the quality and value of academic life itself, a matter that shows up in their relative lack of interest in academic careers. In addition, by treating students as clients instead of colleagues, faculty members place their own research interests at odds with their teaching.

Opportunities for Change

While the unfortunate consequences noted above are not inevitable, they are tied closely to how colleges and universities are organized. With that in mind, moving beyond the curriculum as the sole reference for student academic work may require changes in the organization of colleges and universities.

Some opportunities for this kind of structural change arise through changes in leadership, resources, or the external environment of particular institutions. Others emerge from tensions, ambiguities, and contradictions internal to institutions themselves, either individually or as a group.

One source of internal tension in contemporary institutions of higher education is the ambiguous and problematic relationship between teaching, research, and public service. While this tripartite mission defines the core culture of most colleges and universities, relationships between these three functions are as likely to be competing as to be complementary (Kerr, 1963; Bok, 1982).

This kind of competition exacts an enormous institutional cost. The very functions that frame the organization of academic units, the administration of campus and student services, and the design of curricula are in a state of constant, perilous equilibrium; individual faculty members are subject to continuing challenges about the quality of their contributions in competing domains of activity; programs and projects are developed to defend against abuse rather than to maximize quality and effectiveness; and so on.

While these institutional dysfunctions present obstacles to planned institutional change, the tensions that give rise to them create opportunities for change as well. Within this context, service-learning activities that encourage student participation in teaching, research, and public service can represent a resource of great potential value to faculty, students, and administrators. Presented as such, they may yet prevail.

Conclusion

It seems remarkable that in their efforts to teach students, college and university faculties—the guardians of the curriculum—ignore those contexts and strategies through which faculty members themselves learn best, strategies defined by forms of service learning that depend on actively constructing knowledge and communicating it to others.

Lacking opportunities and encouragement to engage in similar strategies—especially those of teaching and research—students fail to find within the curriculum the foundations of knowledge on which the curriculum is based. With this in mind, general strategies of *reflection*, by themselves, may fail to establish the pedagogical connections we would like to see between service activities and curricula.

As an alternative, Gerald might not only take a course in urban society, but teach a unit within that course about urban poverty. Kathy might investigate how people learn domestic crafts and report on it to her mentors and peers. Stephanie might learn much through teaching some of the law firm's clients how the law library is organized. And from David's involvement in the learning center, he might learn something that could be taught to faculty members, other tutors, or his tutees, for his benefit as well as theirs.

Then, just before they graduate, why not ask these four students to collaborate in designing a course that would communicate to entering students what the undergraduate curriculum is all about, anyway.

Given what we know about faculty members, letting students walk through the curriculum without having to investigate it and explain it to others seems more a disservice than a service, one that colleges and universities—and their students—could do without.

References

Bok, D. *Beyond the Ivory Tower: Social Responsibilities of the University.* Cambridge, Mass.: Harvard University Press, 1982.

Borzak, L. *Field Study: A Sourcebook for Experiential Learning.* Beverly Hills, Calif.: Sage, 1981.

Borzak, L., and Hursh, B. "Integrating the Liberal Arts and Preprofessionalism Through Field Experience: A Process Analysis." *Alternative Higher Education,* 1977, *2* (1), 3–16.

Brown, J. S., Collins, A., and Duguid, P. "Situated Cognition and the Culture of Learning." *Educational Researcher,* 1989, *18* (1), 32–41.

Clark, B. *The Academic Life: Small Worlds, Different Worlds.* Princeton, N.J.: Carnegie Foundation for the Advancement of Teaching, 1987.

Cornwall, M., Schmithals, F., and Jaques, D. (eds.). *Project-Orientation in Higher Education.* Brighton, England: Brighton Polytechnic, 1976.

Cross, P. "A Proposal to Improve Teaching." *Bulletin of the American Association for Higher Education,* 1986, *39* (1), 9–15.

D'Andrade, R. "Three Scientific World Views and the Covering Law Model." In D. Fiske and R. Shweder (eds.), *Metatheory in Social Science.* Chicago: University of Chicago Press, 1986.

Ennis, R. "Critical Thinking and Subject Specificity: Clarification and Needed Research." *Educational Researcher,* 1989, *18* (3), 4–10.

Hursh, B., and Borzak, L. "Toward Cognitive Development Through Field Studies." *Journal of Higher Education,* 1979, *50* (1), 63–78.

Kerr, C. *The Uses of the University.* Cambridge, Mass.: Harvard University Press, 1963.

Kolb, D. *Experiential Learning: Experience as the Source of Learning and Development.* Englewood Cliffs, N.J.: Prentice-Hall, 1984.

Lave, J. *Cognition in Practice.* Boston: Cambridge University Press, 1988.

Little, T. (ed.). *Making Sponsored Experiential Learning Standard Practice.* New Directions for Experiential Learning, no. 20. San Francisco: Jossey-Bass, 1983.

Luce, J. (ed.). *Service Learning: An Annotated Bibliography.* Raleigh, N.C.: National Society for Internships and Experiential Education, 1988.

National Society for Internships and Experiential Education. *Strengthening Experiential Education Within Your Institution.* Raleigh, N.C.: National Society for Internships and Experiential Education, 1986.

Resnick, L. "Learning in School and Out." *Educational Researcher,* 1987, *16* (9), 13–20.

Shils, E. *The Academic Ethic.* Chicago: University of Chicago Press, 1983.

Smelser, N., and Content, R. *The Changing Academic Market.* Berkeley: University of California Press, 1980.

Stanton, T., and Ali, K. *The Experienced Hand: A Student Manual for Making the Most of an Internship.* Cranston, R.I.: Carroll Press, 1982.

Tharp, R. "The Construction of the Teacher-Learner Interaction in the Institutional Context of the School." Paper presented at the American Educational Research Association annual conference, San Francisco, March 27, 1989.

Wagner, J. "Field Study as a State of Mind." In L. Borzak (ed.), *Field Studies: A Sourcebook for Experiential Learning.* Beverly Hills, Calif.: Sage, 1981.

Wagner, J. "Teaching and Research as Student Responsibilities." *Change,* 1987, *19* (5), 26–35.

Jon Wagner is director of University-School Programs and of the Center for Cooperative Education Research at the University of California, Davis. He is the author of Misfits and Missionaries, *an ethnographic study of a school for black, high school dropouts, and editor of* Images of Information, *an examination of the use of still photography in social-science research and teaching.*

*Through an understanding of the concept of servant-
leadership, administrators can integrate community-service
opportunities for all student organizations with the aim of
emphasizing the advantages of nonhierarchical over
hierarchical and power-oriented leadership models.*

The Integration of Service Learning into Leadership and Campus Activities

Cecilia I. Delve, Kathleen L. Rice

For years, student-affairs divisions of universities and colleges have supported students who pursue a portion of their education through non-academic learning opportunities; this participation has often, if not always, included involvement in student organizations and clubs. Also, in the past ten to fifteen years, many institutions of higher education have started to recognize the importance of intentionally developing opportunities to enhance leadership among their student populations. However, these leadership programs have often only taught students in leadership positions, through skill development, how to effectively manage student organizations. Historically,

> leadership skills were once thought a matter of birth. Leaders were born, not made, summoned to their calling through some unfathomable process . . . [At that time, leadership theory] saw power as being vested in a very limited number of people whose inheritance and destiny made them leaders. Those of the right breed could lead; all others must be led. Either you had it or you didn't; no amount of learning or yearning could change your fate [Bennis and Nanus, 1985, p. 5].

Nicoll (1986) writes that today,

> our newest and best approaches to leadership . . . are still rooted in Newton's hierarchic linear and dualistic thinking . . . To our detriment, we still see a leader as one person, sitting at the top of a hierarchy,

determining, for a group of loyal followers, the direction, pace, and outcome of everyone's efforts [p. 30].

The authors of this chapter support a new definition of leadership that challenges every individual, whether or not in a traditional leadership position, to find a way to make a positive difference in the world. By developing and demonstrating qualities of care, courage, ethical sensitivity, responsibility, and the ability to empower others, each person has the potential to have the same impact that is generally assigned to a "leader." It is this form of "leadership" that institutions of higher education need to facilitate in all students, not just in a select few.

By linking community-service and leadership-development opportunities, members and leaders of student organizations can develop themselves as *servant-leaders,* a concept developed by Robert Greenleaf (1977). Greenleaf wrote *Servant Leadership* to express his wish that those who lead first serve.

> The servant-leader *is* servant first . . . It begins with the natural feeling that one wants to serve, to serve *first.* Then conscious choice brings one to aspire to lead. That person is sharply different from one who is *leader* first, perhaps because of the need to assuage an unusual power drive or to acquire material possessions. For such it will be a later choice to serve—after leadership is established. The leader-first and the servant-first are two extreme types. Between them there are shadings and blends that are part of the infinite variety of human nature [p. 13].

Greenleaf goes on to explain that the servant-leader works to serve other people's needs in order to help them grow as persons, to "become wiser, freer, more autonomous, more likely themselves to become servants" [pp. 13–14]. Rather than being demeaning, servant-leadership can be a means of mutually enhancing and empowering all members of an organization, including the group's leader.

By challenging students to develop themselves as servant-leaders, students will learn more than formulas for success. By learning about leadership through community involvement, students have the opportunity to observe a diversity of leaders at work and ask themselves such questions as: How does a person who is homeless mobilize other homeless people to work for change? How does a pregnant teenager overcome many obstacles to be an effective role model for her child? Why does a fifteen-year-old gang member have such a strong, loyal following? What does this teach me about leadership and responsibility in my own life? For what purpose is leadership? For whom is leadership?

Greenleaf (1977, p. 4) asserts that ". . . we live in the age of the anti-leader, and our vast educational structure devotes very little care to nurturing leaders. . . . If there is any influence, formal education seems to discourage such pursuits . . . educators are avoiding the issue when they refuse to give the same care to the development of servant-leaders as they do to doctors, lawyers, ministers, teachers, engineers, scholars." If educators are to play a critical role in the development of ethical, responsible citizens, we cannot discuss the concept of leadership unless we discuss the concept of service.

This chapter outlines strategies for integrating student service in the community with student activities and leadership programs, which include integrating campus activities and leadership programs, integrating leadership into community-service groups, integrating the community into service-learning programs, and finally, applying the Service Learning Model to campus activities. Such a systematic approach is based on a model developed by McManamon, Rice, and Wilson (1988).

Integrating the Servant-Leader Concept into Leadership Programs

By incorporating community service and leadership development for all students involved in campus activities, students will have the opportunity to challenge the traditional assumptions often made about leadership. Also, they will be better prepared to address the difficult issues of leadership and responsibility in their careers, families, and communities during and after their college experience.

The Role of a Campus-Based Leadership and/or Community Service Office. Building community-service opportunities into existing leadership programs does not need to be difficult or expensive. Many campuses have employed full-time staff members to coordinate traditional student-leadership programs or community-service programs. Some colleges and universities, such as Albion College and Seattle University, have hired professionals to develop and coordinate programs that teach the servant-leader concept. A variety of staff members providing leadership development, advisement for student groups, and support for community-service programs can offer an excellent opportunity for collaboration between faculty, staff, and students to raise awareness of, and possible solutions to, issues facing the surrounding community.

The mission of many student organizations includes providing service to the community outside the campus. Such community-service student organizations might include agriculture organizations that provide emergency aid to farmers, sports clubs that assist high school students in developing athletic competencies, or fraternities or sororities that match each member with a child in the community. It is critical that students be aware of, and have available to them, campus resources that can assist them in setting up these types of long- and short-term projects. Appropriately trained and funded community-service and leadership educators can play a valuable role in providing opportunities for students to discuss what they have learned about themselves and the various models of community leadership they have witnessed (Delve, 1989).

Integrating Community-Service and Leadership Programs

There are many opportunities for leadership programs to incorporate community-service experiences into their design. It is critical that these programs be open to all students and not limited to those in traditional leadership positions. Through service-learning opportunities, students can recognize the effect and the difference they can make by serving others and, conversely, allow themselves to be affected and served by the community.

Retreats and Workshops. Many campus-activities offices hold annual retreats, seminars, or workshops. Some of these are for students involved in a variety of campus activities, while others are for more specific populations such as African American students, women, emerging leaders, returning students, international students, and so on. There are many opportunities to incorporate the servant-leader concept into these programs, including workshops on how to get students involved in the community and guest speakers who address the connection between leadership and service.

Creighton University begins their annual leadership retreat with a community-service project. What students learn from this becomes a springboard for discussions throughout the retreat.

In addition to workshops on leadership styles, motivation, and communication, the leadership programs at Southern Illinois University at Edwardsville and North Carolina State University offer several two-hour modules that focus on issues related to community service and ethical development.

At these retreats and workshops, experiential games can challenge students to explore issues of the community. In playing "The Game of Life," students at Ithaca College take on the roles of people who are members of homeless, elderly, disadvantaged-youth groups, and power groups. Each participant plays the game as if he or she were a member of that group. The dialogue that results helps students better understand the perspectives of oppressed populations and challenges them to explore their own values. Likewise, the University of Minnesota's YMCA staff also encourages students to discuss a variety of challenging community issues through a similar game, "The Game of Integrity."

Orientation Programs. Other ways to develop student leadership and civic responsibility may come through orientation programs. For instance, at Azusa Pacific University, through its Bridges Program, student-orientation leaders experience a seven-day plunge into urban life. Working on the premise that "by exposing students to human need and the paradox of that need in a land of plenty . . . their assumptions about others [will] be challenged" (Bunker, 1989, p. 1), students go to San Francisco or Los Angeles to work in soup kitchens and shelters, participate in cleaning and building projects, and assist other service agencies. Additional activities include an opportunity for students to experience what it means to be without practical necessities: During the urban plunge, students are provided with limited financial resources for a day and are told, via a scavenger hunt list, to find food and social services in the city. Ample opportunities exist for students to reflect on their experiences through group discussions and journal writing.

Credit and Noncredit Leadership Courses. Both credit and noncredit courses can provide opportunities for community involvement. Seattle University offers a leadership course where students are challenged to examine their values as they relate to "global realities and local community needs." The University of Vermont includes a panel discussion of community leaders in its leadership course. Such courses also provide an excellent opportunity for students involved on campus to become involved in a course-long community-service project. The class time provides a chance for students to reflect on their experience and discuss its relation to leadership.

The University of Minnesota offers an intense program where 50 students are matched with community or campus leaders. Among other things, the student and mentor meet weekly to discuss the realities of leadership in careers, personal lives, and community involvement. Together, mentors and students participate in two community-service days that emphasize the role of service and leadership.

Recognition. Recognition of students who are involved on campus and in the community is a critical component of servant-leadership programs. The University of Vermont's monthly leadership newsletter includes a regular section highlighting student organizations and individual students who are serving the community. The Office of Community Service Activities at the University of Minnesota presents the Community Service Award, which is presented at the President's Annual Leadership and Service Awards Program. The Campus Compact, a national organization of university and college presidents that seeks to stimulate student participation in voluntary community service (Brozan, 1987), each year recognizes five student leaders through their competitive "Student Humanitarian Award." Recipients of the award are able to donate $1,500 to a program in which they are involved.

"Greek" Organizations and Campus Activities. No chapter on campus activities and community service would be complete without mentioning the long history of philanthropic activities sponsored by fraternities and sororities. As Schmidt and Blaska (1977) describe,

> Greek members themselves see a variety of functions served by their organizations: a home-away-from-home, a place to learn leadership behaviors, an environment for close personal relationships, a milieu of scholastic achievement, [and] a force for community service . . . [p. 164].

Indeed, while many "Greeks" appear to prefer a more nondirect approach to community service (away from the site and the population served), their often creative philanthropic efforts have raised much needed money and awareness for excellent causes. For example, in addition to widely publicized dance marathons and walkathons, some fraternities like Sigma Phi Epsilon at Northern Kentucky University have dribbled a basketball for 18 miles to raise funds for the American Heart Association. The Kansas State University Greek community's "Operation Turkey" raised money and food to donate to a community holiday-food program.

In an effort to have a long-term impact in the community, a member of the Sigma Pi fraternity at Ball State University founded "Greek Vision" in 1986. The "Vision" proposes that each fraternity and sorority in the U.S. and Canada raise dues each month by one dollar. Those extra monies (an estimated $5 million) would be donated to " . . . projects that support a holistic approach [to combat the lack of] food, clothing, shelter, education . . . for immediate relief and for long-term development which [would] work toward a long-term solution to the problem[s]" (Swickard, 1988, p. 13).

Historically, black fraternities and sororities have chosen projects that engage them directly with people in the community. At the University of Maryland, College Park, the Pan Hellenic Council sponsored "Adopting a High School Class," where students assisted the admissions office in its efforts to recruit minority students to college. For two of its community-service activities, Alpha Phi Alpha at the University of Maryland, College Park, provided tutorial services for an elementary school in Washington, D.C., and sponsored "Project Alpha"—a teenage-pregnancy-prevention program for males.

Leadership Development for Community-Service Students

While stimulating a sense of responsibility for the greater community should be an important aspect of all leadership programs and campus activities, it is equally necessary to provide training specifically for those who lead community-service organizations. Students who lead groups that work outside the confines of the "ivory tower" inevitably face different moral, ethical, and cultural issues from those who lead more traditional campus-based groups. These students need the opportunity to develop their leadership skills and styles in order to serve effectively not only the student community but the nonacademic community as well.

Retreats. At Georgetown University, students organize and run the annual Volunteer and Public Service Center Leadership Retreat. Using the theme "From Charity to Justice," students focus on traditional leadership issues, topics of racism and classism, the role of reflection and education in volunteering, and what it means to be a leader in community service. Each year, the Campus Outreach Opportunity League (COOL) offers a weekend-long national conference featuring speakers, workshops, and an opportunity for students to learn from each other about community-service activities at other universities. Through conferences, newsletters, and various resource books, COOL has established itself as a vital source of information for students and administrators who seek to start and develop service organizations on their campuses.

Courses. Even though retreats can be effective in developing leadership capabilities and a sense of civic responsibility, enhancing those skills over a semester-long class can be as, if not even more, effective. For instance, the University of Minnesota's YMCA offers the Metro Internship Program. As stated in the program description, the for-credit program places 25 to 30 students in a ten-week seminar on ethics, leadership, and power in organizations; the seminar is then followed by a full-time, ten-week internship. Metro's purpose is to "have students ask themselves what constitutes right action in the economic, political and social contexts of work, and then test their work with ethical leaders" (Morton, 1988, p. 1).

The University of Vermont's Center for Service-Learning designed a for-credit course in community-service leadership. Through ongoing community service, students were involved in applying the concept of servant-leadership to their own roles as leaders.

Orientation Programs. Orientation programs can be an excellent way to introduce students to a new or deeper understanding of community service. Freshman Orientation to Community Involvement (FOCI) at Georgetown University matches two groups of ten selected freshmen with upperclass leaders, just prior to new student orientation, to explore the needs of Washington, D.C. When freshmen receive their FOCI application they learn that Georgetown places a high priority on community service. For three days, students either paint or refurbish a community agency. Throughout the week, the freshmen, upperclass leaders, and campus and community leaders engage in a series of discussions to explore the problems of the urban poor and to exchange ideas on social responsibility. Many of the freshmen who have participated in FOCI have gone on to become leaders in many of Georgetown's community-service programs.

Involving Community Leaders in Service Programs

Learning about leadership should not be initiated and managed solely by the institution. Often, the people who know most about the community, those who actually live and work in it, are neglected resources of valuable information.

Training. The community can serve as an obvious resource in training and orienting students to the work they will face when they volunteer. Agency supervisors are often very happy to come to campus to educate students about tutoring, health care, or homelessness. These community leaders can also begin to dispel any false assumptions students may have about the community and area of town where they will work.

Invited Speakers. Leadership and civic responsibility are often developed through critical analysis of current issues. Ohio Weslyan University sponsors "The National Colloquium: Linking the Liberal and Civic Arts." The colloquium runs throughout the academic year and brings speakers to campus to address controversial public issues. Likewise, Stanford University sponsors the "You Can Make a Difference" Conference, which annually encourages students to reflect on a particular topic of need and interest to the community. Planned and implemented by students, the Conference encourages students to become knowledgeable in one social area so that they can make choices on how to be effective citizens for change.

Cross-Cultural Exchanges. A challenging way to engage students in work with community leaders is through an international, cross-cultural experience. At Westmont College in Santa Barbara, California, Potter's Clay offers over 350 students an opportunity to spend their spring break working in teams with community and church leaders in Ensenada, Mexico. Potter's Clay was developed to expose students to a third-world culture. In addition to leading vacation Bible schools and evening church services with the assistance of local pastors, students also provide manual labor to construct simple buildings and sponsor basketball and soccer teams to play with local teams. The program has grown so popular that community leaders from the United States now join the students to serve in Mexico. Similar domestic programs at many universities include spring-break programs in Appalachia and Texas.

Community Fairs. An effective way to break down the barriers that may exist between campus and community is to invite community-service agencies to recruit volunteers during the same fair at which student organizations are trying to recruit new members. At The Catholic University of America, agencies from around Washington, D.C., are invited to participate, along with student organizations, in the annual Organizations Fair. Through this and the direct contact with leaders from a variety of agencies, students see that being involved in the community is legitimate, institutionally supported, and co-curricular.

Application of the Service Learning Model

Once one has an understanding of the Service Learning Model, its applications to campus activities and leadership development become evident. Group activities, already described in this chapter, parallel phases one and two, exploration and clarification, and provide a structure that will encourage a student to identify with a particular student organization while also providing a needed service to the community. As students become confident as individuals and with their place in a group, they may be ready to accept a more traditional leadership role within an organization. As leaders and visionaries, such students will experience phase 3, realization, by recognizing their connection with the community and the implications for the campus organization.

Once these leadership qualities have been nurtured, students may experience phase 4, activation, by starting their own organization to meet a particular student and community need. Finally, students who have overcome many obstacles and challenges in their community-service efforts and who have matured as a result of those experiences, may be ready to internalize their experiences and apply them to a life outside the campus. This may come in the pursuit of traditional and nontraditional leadership positions within the community. In addition, students who have experienced service-learning programs within their universities may subsequently be better prepared to serve their communities as agents of change whether they direct a homeless shelter, sit on the board of a health clinic, tutor an illiterate adult, or mentor a child.

Conclusion

It is important to remember that leadership does not always have to follow the traditional power-oriented model to which many of us have become accustomed. As Greenleaf (1977) often suggests, being a *servant-*

leader is the source of true empowerment for all people. Moving a student from an understanding of charity to an understanding of justice often requires a parallel move from the group to a sense of individualism that then translates back to the group and community. It is through this movement that students mature and develop as "whole people" committed to the betterment of the society of which they are a part.

References

Bennis, W., and Nanus, B. *Leaders: The Strategies for Taking Charge.* New York: Harper & Row, 1985.

Brozan, N. "Colleges Encourage Student Volunteers." *New York Times,* January 14, 1987, p. C1.

Bunker, S. "Bridges: A Leadership Training Model with a Volunteer Service Component." Unpublished paper, Azusa Pacific University, Azusa, Calif., 1989.

Delve, C. " 'Green Deans' May Not Be the Ideal Model." *Chronicle of Higher Education,* January 11, 1989, p. B6.

Greenleaf, R. *Servant Leadership.* New York: Paulist Press, 1977.

McManamon, H., Rice, K., and Wilson, S. "Linking Leadership Development and Community Service." Paper presented at the American College Personnel Association National Conference, Miami, Fla., March 21, 1988.

Morton, K. "The Metro Internship Program." Unpublished paper, University of Minnesota, YMCA, 1988.

Nicoll, D. "Leadership and Followership: Fresh Views on an Old Subject." In J. D. Adams (ed.), *Transforming Leadership: From Vision to Results.* Alexandria, Va.: Miles River Press, 1986.

Schmidt, M., and Blaska, B. "Student Activities." In W. Packwood (ed.), *College Student Personnel Services.* Springfield, Ill.: Thomas, 1977.

Swickard, R. "Greek Vision." *Muncie Star,* September 2, 1988, p. 13.

Cecilia I. Delve is director of the Volunteer and Public Service Center at Georgetown University and co-chair of the Service Learning Special Interest Group for the National Society for Internships and Experiential Education. She is president of the Board of Directors for the Calvary Women's Shelter.

Kathleen L. Rice is director of the Student Leadership Program at the University of Minnesota and has also been active in the American College Personnel Association's Commission IV. She is involved with the Minnesota Women's Political Caucus and is a volunteer at St. Joseph's Home for Children and St. Stephen's Shelter in Minneapolis.

*Given the communal nature of residence halls, community
service can be integrated easily into the overall expectations
of resident advisers, hall government, and resident activities
through six enabling conditions.*

Service Learning in the Residence Halls: A Fertile Ground for Student Development

Ronald A. Slepitza

Residence halls traditionally have been identified as environments ripe
with developmental potential. They are settings where students learn to
live together with others very different from themselves, test personal
values, acquire self-discipline, explore future directions, become actively
involved in the campus community, and apply lessons learned in the
classroom to their personal lives (Astin, 1973, 1977; Chickering, 1974;
Feldman and Newcomb, 1969; Riker, 1981; Scott, 1975; Smallwood and
Klas, 1973).

It is precisely because of the richness of this setting that residence
halls offer the ideal environment for the systematic development of service-learning programs. Few student-affairs settings provide an environment as intense, as all encompassing, and as engaging over the long term
as that of residence halls. Few offer the opportunity to pursue student
development in the context of a community that would explicitly use the
interactions within the community as a means to nurture growth.

From the service-learning perspective, the values fostered by ongoing
involvement of students in service-learning activities support the development of the residence-hall community. Residence-hall communities
are built on a foundation of mutual caring that may be nourished by the
student's involvement in service learning. Service-learning programs challenge students to recognize their responsibilities to others and encourage
them to take an active role in serving others. White (1981) has indicated
that volunteer service can be instrumental in developing a capacity for

empathy. Such experiences help the student develop and learn about responsible citizenship as well as promote the development of the residence-hall community. Thus, a symbiotic relationship exists between service learning and the developmental goals of the residence halls.

As important and relevant as this topic is, however, when one searches the literature on service learning or community service as applied to college and university residence halls, one finds a dearth of citations. The results of a recent search of three major databases yielded only three articles that were in any way relevant to this topic. Yet, a conversation with residence-hall administrators revealed that on their respective campuses and in their respective programs many residence halls offer some type of community-service programs or activities. For some of these administrators, there has not been an appropriate medium for sharing information regarding those programs and activities; others may not have had the time or inclination to organize or gather research about such programs in a comprehensive, written form. Clearly, a need exists for more data collection and writing on the topic of service learning and residence halls.

Recently, national attention has focused on the need to improve community-service programs and the experiences of volunteers (*Chronicle of Higher Education,* 1989). This makes the lack of research or writing to guide the development of comprehensive programs even more of a concern. If such programs are to achieve the developmental outcomes that are possible, then considering the components of and the process to establish a systematic, developmentally based approach to service learning is a valuable concern at this time. This chapter explores how such programs can and are being developed in this environment in ways congruent with the Service Learning Model described in Chapter One.

Application of the Developmentally Based Service Learning Model to the Residence Halls

Within the residence halls, one can use the developmentally based model to create a service-learning program that not only utilizes the residence halls well, but also offers a program deliberately designed to promote the personal development of the student engaged in the service learning. The sections that follow explore applications of the phases of the Service Learning Model to the residence halls.

Phase 1: Exploration. Perhaps the most basic level of service-learning programs in the residence halls are those that encourage the resident student to get involved in serving others in a simple, one time, indirect fashion. These programs require little commitment on the volunteer's part, are relatively easy to implement, and are nonthreatening in nature.

There are many examples that can be cited to illustrate the exploration phase; for example, bagging peanuts and raisins for a local soup kitchen, sponsoring a child in Africa, and cleaning up a neighborhood park. A more detailed example is a program implemented in the residence halls at the University of Washington entitled the "Giving Tree" (Reagan, 1988). This program takes place around the Christmas holidays and provides presents to disadvantaged youths from the local community. The student selects a card from the Giving Tree. The card describes an inexpensive Christmas gift wish of a local youth. The person buys and wraps the gift and places it under the Giving Tree where it is anonymously distributed to the youth at a party to which those who have contributed gifts are also invited.

As is true of typical programs in this phase, the "Giving Tree" enables students to experience the value of giving to others without requiring an elaborate investment of time, energy, or money. Such a program offers rewards for students who can see directly the immediate impact of their efforts. Programs like this support the social value of having a sense of responsibility to those around us. This helps the student see that responding to the needs of others is not difficult and can be rewarding.

Programs that fall under the exploration phase are most easily fostered by the active enlistment of the residence-hall floor staff and government to encourage resident students to become involved in a particular service activity. There can easily be residual benefits for the floor, though. Resident advisers (RAs) and floor governors can use involvement in these activities to help their students experience a successful community undertaking that builds floor morale, enhances the sense of floor community, and rewards caring attitudes and behaviors. At this phase in the development of a systematic service-learning program, though, this is not an explicit goal and is not a planned outcome. The key at this phase is choosing an activity that will have a high likelihood of success for both students and organizer and that will not require high levels of energy or commitment from either.

Phase 2: Clarification. In the second phase of a systematically developed approach to service learning, the activities in which the students are engaged spring directly from the students' identification with the floor or the residence-hall community. At this point, floor or building members participate in a variety of different programs or activities that reinforce an individual student's identification with the hall group. There are numerous examples of service programs that have been used by residence-hall staff and student groups to meet this objective. Volunteer work at a shelter, participation in building a house for a low-income family, a visit to the children's wing of a hospital, and organizing and implementing a skating party for a local youth group are examples of such activities.

Important to achievement at this phase in a residence hall is involving students in a variety of activities that permit a number of opportunities to participate. Secondly, the process used to choose which activities to pursue should include the resident students, therefore increasing their commitment to the activity, to service, and to each other. Thus, residence-hall staff and officials should pay as much attention to the decision-making process as to the decision itself. While most rewards will come from the recognition the group gains by its service accomplishments, the skillful planner is wise to build rewarding and enjoyable social experiences into each service activity. These social experiences (for example, after an afternoon at a local children's wing of the hospital, the group goes out to dinner together) enhance the sense of community and build a sense of mutual caring, commitment, and camaraderie between floor members.

Often living in the residence hall is short term, a year being the most for many. People frequently go their separate ways as the second semester of their first year on campus progresses and other involvements take on greater importance. Thus, for many floors, the clarification phase may be the realistic limit to which most members can progress in a systematic service-learning model. In and of itself, the positive experiences gained from these service opportunities, the chance to be involved in a variety of different service activities, and the care and concern that members of the group develop for each other through these activities has enough value. For some members, the positive experiences gained from numerous service activities will lead them to a recognition of the importance service plays in their lives and a desire to pursue involvement in community service in greater depth. For these students, the shift to the realization phase occurs.

Phase 3: Realization. The third phase of the program model describes a period where the student develops a more focused commitment to a particular site, issue, or activity that extends over time. By definition, it represents a more individual orientation and the emergence in the residence hall of community-service leaders. The challenge within the residence hall is helping students maximize their positive experiences at this more committed level and use their talents and experiences to further the development of the service-learning program within the hall.

In helping the student to achieve a positive experience at this level, it is important to provide opportunities for reflection. Providing the student with a faculty member for advice, connecting the person with others who share a similar level of commitment, and providing contact with a community-service coordinator are all important goals to foster this reflection. For these individuals, community often takes on a much different meaning: Their "community" frequently means that group of people with whom they share similar values, experiences, and commitments. This newfound community can be important since it offers the student the opportunity to process experiences with others who have a greater appreciation of the issues and concerns the student now finds significant.

While the student's identification with the primary community changes from the floor to a different group (that is, other volunteers and supervisors), the student's experiences in the service-learning arena, commitment to the value of being involved in community service, and increased level of empathy can be useful in developing a service-learning program within the residence halls: It would be helpful if these students were willing to serve both as mentors for new students at the hall, testing their interest in service, and as reinforcers of the residence-hall tradition of service. In addition, the expertise and experience of these people, with the variety of community-service programs and activities they have pursued, can make staff efforts to implement new programs in subsequent years much easier.

There are challenges for the residence-hall staff member when working within the realization phase. First, it is important to strike a balance between supporting the in-depth involvement of the student in the chosen service area and nurturing this involvement in order to use the student's skills and expertise. Such close attention will help build service learning within the residence-hall system. Secondly, because individuals involved in service are likely to make excellent staff members, careful efforts to encourage their application for residence-hall positions is desirable. Developing a strategy to encourage such applications can be effective in creating and sustaining a residence-hall service-learning program and can enhance the quality of the residence hall staff (Slepitza, 1989).

While one can think of many students who typify those who have arrived at the realization phase, Andrea illustrates the kind of student that one often encounters.

Andrea. Andrea lived in the residence halls for four years, two of them as a residence-hall staff member. She spent her freshman and sophomore years in the residence halls and during that time participated in a variety of community-service programs and activities. Andrea also participated in and helped to organize several retreats for fellow students. During her spring breaks she went on community-service trips offered by the campus to various parts of the country. Over the summers Andrea's commitment to service solidified; she went to the Dominican Republic as part of a summer-long health-oriented service program sponsored by the campus. During Andrea's junior year, she was a resident adviser and was promoted to the position of head resident adviser for her senior year. Because of Andrea's ongoing commitment to service, she was instrumental in developing service opportunities within the residence-hall community, which included organizing the resident adviser staff for their own special service activity. While her personal commitment to service is far reaching, Andrea's commitment to helping others experience service learning has magnified her impact and ensured that her legacy of service carries on in subsequent years.

Andrea is not very different from many who mature in their commitment to serving others. These individuals are often characterized by having higher energy and a need to make a difference. In Andrea's case, her talents have been tapped to help develop the service-learning program of the residence hall.

Phase 4: Activation and Phase 5: Internalization. The activation and internalization phases reflect the movement of the individual to a deeper, personal, all-encompassing level of commitment to service, and to fully embrace the value of service. Such a commitment extends to all facets of one's life as the person strives to be more congruent with the ideals he or she has adopted. This commitment to service becomes a lifestyle and a way of relating to others. It is not often that individuals remain in the residence halls through these two phases. They tend to immerse themselves in a service activity or in the particular community they serve. When they do remain, they can serve as role models for other members of the community. At the same time, it is important to realize that their commitment can be intimidating to others who are testing the waters of involvement.

It is helpful for residence-hall staff to be sensitive to potential conflicts or misperceptions that can emerge at this point. While commitment of this magnitude can be very inspirational to others, students involved in service at this phase may feel isolated and "different." The path they have chosen may not be the path chosen by many. These students may need support that affirms their commitment and helps them come to terms with the inherent differences between the lifestyle and commitments they have chosen and those of their peers. Staff members can help integrate these individuals into the residence social environment and encourage others to appreciate their commitment by offering programs on the floor about service, referring students to organizations that match their interests, and ensuring a location for informal discussions.

Two programs illustrate the efforts that can be made by residence-hall staff to foster service learning at these higher levels of involvement. The *District Action Project* of Georgetown University involves residents of a co-ed floor in a program sponsored by the Department of Resident Life and the Volunteer and Public Service Center. Students apply to live on this service-learning floor; once accepted, program participants volunteer five to seven hours per week at a community-service organization of their choice. Students are placed with a service agency that directly benefits residents of the District of Columbia. Program participants meet weekly in small groups to discuss their experiences, support each other's involvement, and reflect on learning and insights gained. Annual retreats and special projects enable students to explore issues about themselves and the community that they have had to confront. This program allows students to become deeply involved in community service, establishes a community of residents who share similar commitments, and provides a forum where the students can reflect on and integrate their experiences.

The second program originated at the College of Wooster in Wooster, Ohio. Thirty houses, accommodating between five and thirty-five students each, surround the campus and form the backbone of this service-learning residential program. Students apply to a particular house as a group and in their application propose a service-learning project that will be the focus of their efforts for the year. Each resident may spend four to six hours per week in a service project that responds to community or college needs. Each house has a faculty or staff adviser who assists the house in meeting program needs. Further, a volunteer network, coordinated by the Career Development Center, has been established. The contact people from each house comprise the network, which meets monthly and arranges budgetary and logistical support for the houses. From this effort, students develop a strong commitment to the service organization and to each other. Continuity over the years has developed as particular houses continue with the service projects of the previous years. The community of Wooster relies on the assistance of this core of committed volunteers and sees this source of assistance as an important way to bring the city and college together.

Progress Through the Phases

Viewing the application of the Service Learning Model in the residence-hall environment, one sees that service-learning activities may be used to build community involvement and to foster a caring community. As these activities become more numerous, service becomes an accepted value. With increased commitment, individuals shift their attention to forming a community with those with whom they share common values. The task for the residence-hall staff is to consider carefully the knowledge, skills, and experiences of students already involved in service; this will help encourage service by students in the residence hall and ensure program continuity from year to year. Since the already involved individuals have demonstrated a commitment to others, this task will not be difficult if they also feel some sense of responsibility for the service-learning program that is being developed within their residence halls. The inevitable challenge for the residence-hall administrator is to provide the necessary resources to enable an ongoing, comprehensive service-learning program.

Enabling Conditions for Promoting Service-Learning Programs in Residence Halls

Service-learning programs must not be haphazard if they are to contribute both to the development of the student and to the residence-hall community. Nor are such programs likely to have a long-term impact on the residence-hall environment without careful attention to their planning and implementation. In order to establish a service-learning program as suggested by the Service Learning Model, several enabling conditions ought to exist.

A clear acknowledgement of the value of community service should be articulated by the residence-hall administration. A clear commitment on the part of residence-hall administrators, staff, and hall government to community service must be evident to students. The more this is evinced both in the words and actions of the administration, the easier it will be to develop a comprehensive service-learning program.

Recognition and rewards for those active in service-learning programs should be visible. When involvement in community service is recognized as a valid leadership experience, when those most involved in such programs can stand alongside other outstanding residence-hall leaders, when such involvement is valued as a key precursor experience that aids in the acquisition of residence-hall student staff positions and hall-governance positions; then service-learning programs will be seen as an integral educational component of the residence-hall experience. A service-award program in the form of a reception or banquet, sponsored by the hall government, that recognizes outstanding contributions to the neighboring community is an excellent way to ensure visibility.

Through recognition and rewards, one may be able to improve the quality of the residence-hall staff and government. Astin (1977) and White (1981) have identified increased empathy as one of the outcomes of involvement in community service. Given the importance of empathy to the peer-helper relationship (Delworth, Sherwood, and Casaburi, 1974), the active enlistment of those who demonstrate care and concern for others could improve the quality of the living environment. At the author's institution, a comparison was conducted of residents' appraisal of resident advisers' performance, where resident advisers were classified as being either highly, moderately, or little involved in community-service activities. The highly involved RAs were seen by their residents as having taken a greater interest in them, encouraging programs, and increasing the students' participation in floor programs (Slepitza, 1989). While few conclusions can be drawn from a single study at one institution, it is possible that the staffing goals of the residence-hall system may be furthered by recognizing those more fully involved in community service.

Inclusion of community service in resident-adviser training sends a clear, strong message that volunteerism is an integral component of campus community living. Including community service in resident-adviser training will not only send a clear message to the staff, but will also encourage creative ways to integrate service into the programs of the residence-hall community. Involving the campus volunteer-coordinator in the resident-adviser training will establish an important relationship and the necessary framework from which to proceed. For example, using the Service Learning Model as the basis for training about community service, a greater understanding of the limits of programming with and for the resident advisers' floor will be gleaned. Going one step further, incorporating a service project into resident adviser training will provide the hands-on experience likely to motivate RAs to enter community service.

Publicity, logistical, and budgetary support for service-learning programs will further the establishment of a systematic service program. Well-developed service-learning programs are well advertised. Within the residence halls, such advertising should be directed primarily to the floor community. Logistically, adequate resources should be devoted to developing easy entry for the student into the program. This can be fostered primarily by the resident adviser or hall governor; for example, arranging for transportation to the community-service setting or offering carry-out meals when such involvement takes the student away from campus over the meal hour. Finally, in order for service-learning programs to be an integral part of the residence-hall educational program they should receive explicit budgetary support, to include monies for retreats, necessary supplies, transportation costs, program advertisement, and more.

Support for service-learning programs is furthered by involving others in program development and decision making. Committees should be established to facilitate the maintenance and expansion of the service-learning program. These committees ideally should include residence-hall staff and students, faculty, other members of the college or university, and members of the external community. This advisory committee can play a vital role in determining program direction, expanding service opportunities, and soliciting the business community for financial support and in-kind service contributions. The more a shared commitment to service learning is developed by many constituencies, the more likely these programs will grow.

Faculty involvement facilitates service-learning program development. As a direct link is established between residence-hall students in the service-learning program and faculty members in disciplines related to the service-learning project, it will be easier to bridge the gap between the formal lessons of the classroom and their practical application. To ensure this link, the residence hall might sponsor a lecture series by faculty involved in community service, thus providing role models. One-on-one tutorials might be set up between faculty members and students to discuss, on a more personal level, the academic connection with the student's service activity. The residence hall might encourage faculty to "adopt" a floor and lead weekly discussions about various community issues.

The identification of supportive faculty members who share an interest in community service and see these experiences as an asset to the student's development is valuable for three reasons. First, the deliberate involvement of faculty in the service-learning program can greatly enhance the opportunities for the student to reflect upon experiences gained. Such reflection helps students integrate their experiences and personalizes their learning. Second, faculty might be more inclined to offer academic credit for the student's experience, thus adding another incentive. Finally, when students see faculty members who evince a commitment to service, it demonstrates more fully that such actions are a reasonable expectation of members of a community.

While faculty involvement is important to any service-learning program, their participation is especially important within the residence halls. Excellent residence-hall systems rely on broad-based support to extend their programs and services beyond providing the basic services of clean, safe, comfortable, orderly environments to supporting academic and personal development. The more faculty are involved in residence-hall educational and developmental programs, the greater will be their appreciation of and support for the community role that residence halls play.

Assessment of the developmental impact of service-learning programs as part of the residence-hall evaluation process further helps substantiate the quality of the residence-hall programs. Much can be gained by demonstrating the developmental progress of residents who are involved in community service. Measuring the ability of such students to be empathic, to understand and appreciate differences, and to articulate the role of a responsible citizen can provide supportive evidence to justify on-campus residency requirements.

Together, these enabling mechanisms can be valuable tools to build a stronger residence-hall service-learning program. The more they are used together, the greater the likelihood of a program's success. A program that awards the student's commitment to community service, recognizes his or her accomplishments, helps the student to test academic and career plans in the light of community service, and offers academic, logistical, and budgetary support for such efforts has a much greater chance of appealing to a wider range of students than a more narrowly defined program. If only considered from the perspective of involving more students in service learning, it is important, according to Fitch (1987), to use an approach that respects both altruistic and egoistic motivations when reviewing the characteristics and motivations of college students active in community service.

If we are to be true to our commitment to helping students become responsible citizens, then we must establish effective programs that assist students in learning from and experiencing the benefits of performing service for others. Such programs promise to aid us in meeting the educational and developmental potential of residence halls.

References

Astin, A. *Four Critical Years: Effects of College on Beliefs, Attitudes, and Knowledge.* San Francisco: Jossey-Bass, 1977.

Astin, A. "The Impact of Dormitory Living on Students." *Educational Record,* Summer 1973.

"Bush Proposes $25-Million to Coordinate Community-Service Efforts." *Chronicle of Higher Education,* June 28, 1989, p. 14.

Chickering, A. W. *Commuting Versus Resident Students: Overcoming Educational Inequities of Living Off Campus.* San Francisco: Jossey-Bass, 1974.

Delworth, U. G., Sherwood, G., and Casaburi, N. *Student Paraprofessionals: A Working Model for Higher Education.* Student Personnel Series no. 17. Washington, D.C.: American College Personnel Association, 1974.

Feldman, K. A., and Newcomb, T. M. *The Impact of College on Students.* Vol. 1: *An Analysis of Four Decades of Research.* San Francisco: Jossey-Bass, 1969.

Fitch, R. T. "Characteristics and Motivations of College Students Volunteering for Community Service." *Journal of College Student Personnel,* 1987, *28,* 424–431.

Reagan, J. "The Giving Tree: Successful Collegiate Community Service." Paper presented at the 40th Annual Conference of the Association of College and University Housing Officers–International, July 12, 1988.

Riker, H. C. "Residential Learning." In A. W. Chickering and Associates (eds.), *The Modern American College: Responding to the New Realities of Diverse Students and a Changing Society.* San Francisco: Jossey-Bass, 1981.

Scott, S. "Impact of Residence Hall Living on College Student Development." *Journal of College Student Personnel,* 1975, *16* (3), 214–219.

Slepitza, R. A. *Involvement in Community Service as a Predictor of Resident Advisor Performance.* Omaha, Neb.: Department of Residence Life, Creighton University, 1989.

Smallwood, F. D., and Klas, L. "A Comparison of the Academic, Personal, and Social Effects of Four Different Types of University Residential Environments." *Journal of College and University Student Housing,* 1973, *3* (2), 13–19.

White, R. W. "Humanitarian Concern." In A. W. Chickering and Associates (eds.), *The Modern American College: Responding to the New Realities of Diverse Students and a Changing Society.* San Francisco: Jossey-Bass, 1981.

Ronald A. Slepitza is associate vice-president for student services at Creighton University in Omaha, Nebraska. He has worked with residence-hall programs for the past twelve years.

The Service Learning Model is complemented by Parks's,
Westerhoff's, and Fowler's faith-development models, as well
as by the social-justice activities of campus ministries' staffs.

Grounded in Justice: Service Learning from a Faith Perspective

Erin D. Swezey

> I thought my experience of working with women and
> children would be different than it was. I found that every-
> one has the same needs and same desires in life. We may
> have different ways of living, yet the dignity of each person
> is important. My service experience has caused me to look
> at my directions and recheck my priorities . . . I have
> learned to listen . . . God speaks to me through others.
> —Student reflection, Seattle University, 1989

The above quotation exemplifies reflections shared by students after participating in community-service experiences coordinated and sponsored
by their campus' religious organizations. Many students express that they
have experienced transformations of their attitudes, values, and hearts.
Some express feelings of being uncomfortable or of being inspired. Some
pose questions about larger issues of social justice that they have encountered. Some describe experiences of discovering a common ground of
humanity, human dignity, or God or an Ultimate Being in their service.
All are attempting to create meaning from their experiences, and all have
been shaped or transformed by those meanings. Making meaning out of
lived experiences is an ongoing dynamic within one's spiritual or "faith"
development. This chapter explores how community service within campus religious life can encourage, support, and challenge students' spiritual development, and in particular, the development of faith, during
their college experience.

NEW DIRECTIONS FOR STUDENT SERVICES, no. 50, Summer 1990 © Jossey-Bass Inc., Publishers

In college, students self-consciously begin to reflect on the meaning of life itself. "Never before and never again in the life cycle is the same constellation of forces available to enable the formulation of life-transforming vision . . . (it) is a vital opportunity given to every generation for the renewal of human life" (Parks, 1986, p. 86). Service-learning programs sponsored and coordinated by campus ministries can provide this vital opportunity for the formulation of one's life-transforming vision and recomposition of a sense of life's meaning or faith. At a time when much is being discussed and written about the missing dimension of wellness models or student-development theory in terms of our educational responses and programs addressing students' spiritual or faith development, promoting student involvement in campus-ministry-sponsored community-service programs is one avenue to meet this need.

The most effective and authentic campus-ministry community-service opportunities are grounded in a social-justice context that promotes direct service, social analysis, and structural change. This foundation in social justice requires that community service from a faith perspective move beyond charity and address the root causes that create the need for service within our society and world. Within this service, transforming relationships can develop that affect one's core values and beliefs about self, others, world, and God or an Ultimate Being. Community service, no doubt, is a social and human good; however, those involved in such service yearn for the spiritual belief out of which such service comes naturally and on which, if it is to be lasting, this service must rest (Healy, 1985). The integration of service-learning within the campus ministry promotes both an active faith and the discovery of one's faith through action.

The Evolution of Service in Campus Ministries

Community service is indigenous to the history of religious life on college campuses. During colonial times institutions of higher education were established based on a religious commitment and "the common belief that the future of the new society depended on having educated clergy and public leaders" (Butler, 1989, p. 4). In the mid-nineteenth century, the Young Men's and Women's Christian Associations (YMCAs and YWCAs, respectively) were established to develop Christian leadership among students as well as to provide community and campus service. An outgrowth of the campus "Y" movement was the student volunteer movement, which promoted service and global consciousness. Although today "Y's" have a less prominent role in higher education, Butler indicates that "they remain an important link to our history and a strong voice for inclusiveness, human rights, and community building within a framework of global justice" (p. 5). During the 1960s, religious-life programs at both public and private institutions began to focus on service to others and global concerns of peace and justice. Today, the diversity of denominational presence and campus-ministry models varies as much as the different kinds of institutions of higher education. Thus, the existence, extent, mission, and comprehensiveness of service learning within religious life and campus ministries also varies according to ministry models, resources, and denominational goals.

Faith-Development Models

Before describing effective components of service-learning opportunities within campus ministries and highlighting specific service programs that have been effective in supporting and promoting the development of the faith, we will review three models of such development. We will then draw parallels between the models and the components of the Service Learning Model.

Important to the discussion of faith development is the definition of faith. According to theorists Westerhoff (1976), Fowler (1987), and Parks (1986), faith is more than religion or belief. Faith is manifest in action, is integral to all human life, and is something that all human beings do (Parks, 1986). Faith is the dynamic process of making meaning of our experiences. "Faith is the very mode through which the person shapes new self-understandings and new orientations toward the world" (Chamberlain, 1988, p. 9). Sharon Parks (1986) defines faith in more poetic terms: "Faith is not only the act of setting one's heart, it is also what one sets one's heart upon" (p. 26).

Westerhoff's Styles of Faith. Westerhoff (1976) presents four styles of faith: experienced, affiliative, searching, and owned. *Experienced faith* involves expressing and understanding faith through interactions with others, based upon exploring and testing, observing and copying, imagining and creating, experiencing and reacting. These behaviors parallel those found in students who are in the exploration phase of the Service Learning Model.

The *affiliative* style of faith involves belonging to and participating in a community of faith. Affiliative faith also responds to or evokes one's affective realm; it is often called "religion of the heart." Affiliative faith parallels the clarification phase of the Service Learning Model.

Searching faith has three characteristics: doubting, questioning or critical judgment of earlier faith beliefs, experimentation with alternatives and other traditions, and commitment to persons and causes. Initially, such commitments within a searching faith can change constantly and contradict prior commitments. This journey reflects the realization phase of the Service Learning Model.

Owned faith leads one to personal and social action. There is an integration of faith both in word and in deed, challenging one to witness this faith through service; such behavior is found in those who are in the activation or internalization phase of the Service Learning Model.

Fowler's Stages of Faith. Aided by developmental theorists Kohlberg and Piaget, James Fowler's (1987) research on the development of faith formulates six stages of faith. Fowler's stages three through five are most relevant to college students and the Service Learning Model and therefore will be described below. Typically, college students move from *conventional faith* (stage three) through the *individuative/reflective stage* (stage four); some students, particularly older adults, begin the *conjunctive phase* (stage five). Similar to Westerhoff's styles of faith, these three stages of faith development can be linked to the five phases of the Service Learning Model.

Central to conventional faith is the capacity for mutual interpersonal relationships. Affiliation with others is paramount, thus conformity of values, beliefs, and commitments predominates. The group shapes the individual's sense of meaning and faith. Since conformity to the group is so strong, values and beliefs are largely unexamined. This stage of faith development matches the exploration and clarification phases of the Service Learning Model in which group identity and structured, nonthreatening activities are encouraged.

Movement to individuative/reflective faith involves the critical examination and questioning of the value and belief systems previously held and never before questioned. This process of examination is often painful and prolonged. One's reflective abilities dramatically increase. There is more congruence between and authenticity about one's values, beliefs, community affiliations, and actions. Given this capacity to step back from one's own perspective and the perspective of one's own group, one can more readily embrace diversity and the experience of those who have been oppressed. Exposure to broader norms of justice, compassion, love, and dignity also occurs. Because community service influences faith development and, reciprocally, growth in faith enables personal development in service learning, students possessing an individuative/reflective faith will participate within the realization and activation phases of service. Students confronting issues of diversity are less influenced by their peer group and more consistent in their values and lifestyle.

Movement to conjunctive faith is evident as one struggles with the paradoxes of the world; that is, a world in which both good and evil, oppressor and oppressed exist. One begins to make peace with the tension arising from the realization that truth must be approached from a number of different directions and angles of vision. One's faith becomes more contemplative in nature. A stronger commitment to social justice, which transcends class, race, and religious bias, is evident. Hence, the conjunctive faith stage corresponds directly to phase five, internalization, of the Service Learning Model.

Throughout all these stages, Fowler believes that the context of community is essential to the forming of faith. He also believes that as one gradually develops, one's reflective consciousness or ability to participate in various kinds of self-reflection also develops. Finally, as one moves from one stage to the next, there is a steady widening in social or other-oriented perspective taking. Thus, sense of community, reflective consciousness, and social awareness can be enhanced uniquely by service-learning programs within campus ministries or campus religious life.

Parks's Model for Faith. Sharon Parks's (1986) research has built on Fowler's stages of faith as well as drawn on the human development theories of Gilligan, Kegan, Keniston, Kohlberg, and Piaget. In her research with college students, she has identified a specific faith-development phase between Fowler's conventional faith and individuative/ reflective stage (stages three and four, respectively) that is relevant to service learning. Parks asserts that students' probing commitment, their mentors or role models, ideologically compatible communities, and images, symbols, and ideologies are significant components of the faith-development process. Similar variables of challenge and support within the Service Learning Model promote the student's transition between phases of social awareness, from the sense of the individual to that of the global community.

Parks maintains that college students possess a unique capacity to critically conceptualize the ideal. The developmental process of the student is a search for the ideal or an envisioning of a dream that adequately and with integrity grounds and shapes the relationship between one's emerging self and the complex world. Cognitively, one explores and tests possible truths and visions, warily and tentatively weighing their congruence with one's experience of self and the world. Parks calls this exploration and critique, *probing commitment.*

In this period of exploration and critique, college students have feelings of power, promise, and hope, yet they are also vulnerable to disappointment, despair, and a sense of powerlessness. Parks suggests that *mentors* can serve as a transforming power or mediating guide in this specific faith-developing process.

Very powerful in this phase of faith development is the need for a network of belonging members or community. Parks believes that community is critical to the support and encouragement of students' searching, questioning, emerging, promising, and vulnerable selves. She asserts that *ideologically compatible communities* are essential to confirm the faith that an individual is reconstructing during this time. As students try to make meaning of the world, to integrate diversity and new truths, and to maintain an ideal sense of vision, the community "promises a place of nurture" (Parks, 1986, p. 89).

Finally, Parks believes that in order for college students to continue to mature in their faith, more than exploring truths, choosing mentors and participating in community is needed. Using Gilligan's research, Parks observes that "the structure of young adult faith mandates a search for an 'authentic' basis for moral action and that this search can be fulfilled by 'contents' as diverse as hedonism, cynical oral nihilism, or an ethic of service to others . . ." (1986, p. 105). Therefore, faith development is shaped also by *images, symbols,* and *ideologies.* Parks's review of Gilligan's research notes that those students most able to struggle definitively and responsibly with moral dilemmas believe in human dignity and respect and possess a sense of obligation to respond to and alleviate human suffering and injustice. She believes that if students are offered images that require an ongoing struggle with "otherness," then they are more likely to continue maturing in forms of faith. Community-service opportunities can offer diverse experiences to enable students to continue this ongoing struggle with "otherness."

Comprehensive service-learning programs coordinated by campus ministries address the major components of these models of faith development. Opportunities are thereby given for affiliation, community development, and ideologically compatible communities and experiences are designed to promote the reflective consciousness, critical analysis, and probing commitment of students' searching faith. Students encounter much diversity and develop relationships with others "like me but not like me," thus promoting increased social awareness. Campus ministers, community-resource people, experienced student leaders, and peer-reflection groups serve to provide role models and mentors to support and mediate between ideal perceptions and lived experience. With the addition of images, symbols, and reflective processes focusing on social justice, faith development is encouraged, leading students from faith in action, beyond charity, to a lifelong response to alleviating human suffering and injustice.

Integrating Campus-Ministry Programs with the Service Learning Model

The Service Learning Model described in Chapter One is compatible with community service based upon the above models of faith development. These models have clear parallels with one another and demonstrate similar, supporting developmental transitions and phases. Community-service programs within campus ministries exemplify the integration of these models of faith development and service learning.

The effective and established programs of community service within campus-ministry settings are comprehensive. Such programs offer opportunities for *direct service* within community agencies or programs, involvement with *advocacy or social-justice organizations* (Amnesty International, Bread for the World, Pax Christi, and local, campus committees that sponsor educational programs and encourage active responses to social problems), *immersion experiences* (intensive inner-city experiences and international service with the poor in third-world countries), and *campus programs* that bring local communities together with the college or university community (senior-citizen dances, children's fairs). They also offer events that involve the entire campus annually (hunger-awareness weeks, food and clothing drives, global-justice symposiums). Similar to the Service Learning Model, this variety of opportunities allows for nondirect, indirect, and direct involvement, for a diversity of entry points to enable student involvement, for different levels of commitment among students, and for different goals and challenges. These include initial exposure, encountering diversity, and developing faith dedicated to service. The Service Learning Model provides campus-ministry professionals with a structure and description of the means to promote the development of faith in their students.

Examples of Campus-Ministry Service Programs. Some of the service opportunities coordinated by campus ministries at Emory University, Oxford (Georgia), Loyola Marymount University (Los Angeles, California), Seattle University (Washington), and Western Washington University (Bellingham, Washington) are highlighted and include references regarding where these programs fit into the phases of the Service Learning Model.

Direct Service. Ninth Street School Community Project, sponsored jointly by the Los Angeles Unified School District and Loyola Marymount's Campus Ministry, provides on-campus recreational programs for the low-income children of this elementary school. Students plan special campus events which include celebrating holidays and organizing community outings to entertainment parks. Some of these students student-teach within the elementary school, and others develop special "brother" or "sister" relationships with children from the recreational programs. This program exemplifies how campus-ministry service can be "institutionalized" within the college or university setting.

Prison Ministry with the Concerned Lifers Organization brings together students and staff members from Seattle University's Campus Ministry with incarcerated members of the Concerned Lifers Organization of the state's reformatory. Quarterly, student leaders, campus ministers, and inmate officers of the Lifers Organization meet to plan discussion topics for the bimonthly visits and to discuss concerns and ideas for improving the prison ministry encounters between students and University staff and the inmates. Students and inmates gather in large and small groups for two hours of community building and discussion on topics that include current events, personal growth, and the prison reform system. For the students, reflection opportunities occur immediately after each visit and in biquarterly, structured evening sessions.

Trinity United Methodist Church's Night Shelter and *Habitat for Humanity* are two service programs sponsored by Emory University, Oxford in Georgia. Through the former, students travel forty miles into Atlanta twice a week for all-night shifts providing shelter and job assistance for homeless individuals. The latter, Habitat for Humanity, is a project held every Saturday where students help low-income families build permanent low-income housing. The impetus for Emory-at-Oxford's service programs grew from the Oxford Christian Fellowship, which discusses issues of poverty, racism, sexuality, and nuclear disarmament within a faith context. A desire grew among the fellowship students to put their faith into action. Thus, *Oxford Outreach* was established to enable students to organize and participate in community service. Participation that allows the people served to use their own resources and talents to shape their destinies is crucial to Emory-at-Oxford's programs.

The direct-service programs described span the Service Learning Model as examples of phases two through four (clarification, realization, and activation). The Ninth Street School Community Project offers the kind of program structure needed at phase two, and the Prison Ministry with the Concerned Lifers Organization integrates campus-ministry reflection sessions, typically given at phases three or four. The Trinity United Methodist Church's Night Shelter and Habitat for Humanity are solid examples of phase three or phase four interventions. The students involved in these programs evidence the advocacy component of the Service Learning Model's phase four.

Advocacy/Social-Justice Organizations. Historically, many campus ministries have been the home for campus committees, involving students, faculty, and staff, that educate the campus community about social and global issues and empower that community to act on them. Both Loyola Marymount and Seattle University sponsor *Amnesty International* groups, which focus on human-rights violations throughout the world. Seattle University's *Bread for the World* committee promotes hunger awareness (through sponsorship of educational events and speakers) and, through letter-writing campaigns, lobbies Congress for legislation supporting food and economic-justice programs. Loyola Marymount's campus ministry also supports a student group called *Today Not Tomorrow (TNT)*. This group emerged to study questions about why so much hunger exists in the world. In their reflection, these students examined the root causes of social problems and became involved in efforts at social change within their local community. They also became involved in direct-service projects such as food and clothing drives and working with street youth. All of these campus organizations are avenues for students to learn more about issues, especially those related to their service experience, and to stand in solidarity with those people with whom they serve.

A student's reasons for involvement in an advocacy or social-justice organization will vary. Therefore, these organizations' activities might offer for one student the supports and challenges of phase two (clarification) and for another student, those of phase four (activation). For example, for the less active student, involvement in Amnesty International might only involve writing an occasional letter of protest, while for the student who has been to El Salvador and worked with oppressed people, involvement will more likely be greater. In fact, the more socially conscious student will probably be involved in Amnesty International as a supplement to other direct-service activities.

Immersion Experiences. Given faith traditions that promote reflection and retreat, many campus ministries sponsor retreat-like immersion experiences to provide students with exposure to, and fuller experiences of, inner-city life and third-world countries. Urban plunges and inner-city retreats challenge students to gain a broad understanding of the social needs and issues in their local community. Direct-service work with homeless, refugee, and senior-citizen populations enables students to develop relationships that can continue in on-going service. Presentations by community coordinators, reflection and prayer, and community meals are powerful supports for these immersion experiences. Both Emory-at-Oxford's and Loyola Marymount's campus ministries have international equivalents. Each offers programs that travel to Mexico and provide services in orphanages. Emory-at-Oxford's immersion experience lasts for two to three weeks and includes meetings with political, cultural, educational, and religious leaders. Also available are summer internships that allow students to remain for extended time periods. Loyola Marymount sponsors *Los Niños' Retreats,* which are weekend immersion experiences that bring students into direct contact with the realities of poverty in the third world. Students maintain relationships with the children they meet through on-going visits, letters, and special campus events that bring the children to Los Angeles.

The Shalom Center, the ecumenical campus ministry center at Western Washington University, sponsored a similar Los Niños program during one spring break. Spending the week in Tijuana, students either worked at an orphanage or built a house for the community. This immersion experience was a joint ecumenical venture that brought students and ministers of different faith traditions together in service. Upon return, the students compiled a book about their experiences, reflecting on the many transformations they experienced of heart, mind, and spirit.

Immersion experiences can vary greatly in structure, so as to appeal to a variety of students. For instance, Western Washington University's Tijuana experience might provide an excellent initial service opportunity for the student who has had limited exposure to social-justice issues. By offering a highly organized week-long group activity, the less involved student has the needed support of a group. The experience can be nondirect (at the site, but with no direct contact with the client community), thereby providing a nonthreatening intervention. Intensive experiences, such as the ones in Mexico, sponsored by Emory-at-Oxford and Loyola Marymount, are more likely geared toward the politically and socially aware student. With the inclusion of an educational component in the direct-service experience, the immersion experience follows closely along the lines of phase four (activation) or phase five (realization).

Campus-Wide Programs. Many campus ministries also coordinate annual events that involve the entire campus community. Some of these events bring disenfranchised individuals or communities to campus for a campus-immersion experience. Others are events more educational in nature with some service component. Examples of the latter are hunger-awareness weeks and social-justice conferences. Loyola Marymount sponsors a *Life and Peace Week,* which provides the university community with five days of speakers, films, panel discussions, and activities co-sponsored by all the campus's social justice organizations. Seattle University's Campus Ministry, together with the local L'Arche communities (Christian communities for differently-abled adults), coordinate a three-day experience called *Sharing Our Hearts* in which L'Arche community members and their staff assistants, from all over the United States and Canada, live with students. Classroom presentations, social and recreational events, community meals, reflection, and worship comprise an experience that can build lasting relationships.

Programs designed on campus can serve students well in supporting transitions from one developmental phase to another. It is through these educational activities that students are challenged to take a hard look at the social issues that surround them. While students are challenged by what they learn, they are supported by the safe environment of the campus.

Service Learning with a Faith Foundation of Justice

Both the Hebrew and Christian scriptures provide rich, empowering traditions that call for the faithful to perform acts of justice. As evidenced by the campus-ministry programs described above, community service embracing the demand for justice dedicates itself to four components: *sufficient and basic life goods* (food, shelter, clothing, health care, skills development, work), *human dignity and esteem* (recognizing, affirming, and calling forth the value of each person and community), *participation* (the right of individuals and peoples to shape their own destinies), and *solidarity* (the corresponding duty to promote these rights with and for others) (McGinnis, 1984). Given these components, service-learning programs coordinated by campus-ministry organizations directly involve students with the needs and issues of those disenfranchised; that is, of individuals and communities without economic, cultural, and political power or advocates in our local communities, country, or world.

Paramount to the quest for justice is the building of authentic relationships between students and the individuals and communities with whom they serve. These relationships affirm the reciprocal learning inherent in service. Service in this context is not a doing to or for but a serving with a person or group; enabling and empowering disenfranchised individuals and communities to be "agents of their own development and not just the beneficiaries of someone else's efforts" (McGinnis, 1984, p. 43). Together, the students and the individuals or communities being served plan and carry out the community-service experience. The task of the service becomes secondary to the relationships that develop within the service experience. The students receive as well as give. This leads to a deeper understanding of faith and empowers students to create more equitable situations for those people with whom they serve and to make the connections between many of the issues of injustice (for example, poverty, war, racism, sexism) within our world.

Occasions for Reflection

The faith-development theorists believe that faith is the dynamic process of making meaning of our lived experience. Service-learning programs within the context of a campus ministry provide students with the opportunity for reflection; that is, with the time to step back from their experiences, listen, ponder, analyze, express feelings and insights, and become aware of and begin to understand the centrality of service grounded in justice. Given religious and ministerial education, campus ministers are uniquely suited to offer programs that facilitate these reflection opportunities. In the Service Learning Model, reflection is integrated after the second phase; therefore, most of the service-learning programs within campus ministries support phases two, three, four, and five of the Service Learning Model.

Reflection can occur in many ways during the service experience. Initially, during exploration meetings with campus ministers to determine interest areas, service opportunities, and individual commitment, students learn about the diversity of human and community need and discern how they might serve most effectively. Often, as part of the service experience, students have opportunities for immediate reflection and sharing of their experiences in their peer groups. These immediate experiences of reflection make possible the "teachable moments," when students share difficult encounters or profound insights with one another. Over time, structured reflection groups provide opportunities for students to grapple with their faith, to see the justice issues that relate to the problems of those whom they serve, and to be empowered to move to further levels of action. The latter kind of reflection embodies Parks's concept of "ideologically compatible communities," which are essential for students to integrate diversity and new perspectives encountered within their experiences.

As students intensify their service experience, structured group reflections directly address the connection between service and justice within the context of faith. A graphic introduction to this concept is a model entitled "The Two Feet of Christian Service" (McGinnis, 1984), which depicts one step of direct service (helping people survive) and the other step of social change (removing the causes that create the problems of disenfranchised people and communities). Given their service experiences and relationships, students can understand and discuss the root causes and issues that create unjust economic, political, or cultural situations. Together, in these reflection groups, students are able to plan options and actions that will further their education about social issues, which will lead to political and social action in support of specific issues, create changes in their personal lifestyles, and mobilize the campus community to a new level of awareness. For many students, linking these reflections and social actions directly to the Judeo-Christian scriptures is paramount.

As Parks and Fowler attest, these reflection times are the key opportunities for students to create meaning from their experiences and to shape their own perspectives and be shaped by others' perspectives. Often students who get involved with service, oblivious to any connection between service and faith, discover the dynamic of faith within their lives from these opportunities to reflect upon their experiences. Other students who are more grounded in their faith discover deeper meanings and move to new levels of faith related to values and commitments to social justice.

Opportunities and Cautions

Given the natural inclination of religious-life organizations to gather students in fellowship, prayer, and reflection, and campus ministers' expertise in providing different kinds of service experiences, service-learning opportunities sponsored by campus ministries are a rich resource for the development of faith and values of college students as well as for education about social and global concerns. Campus ministries can improve these service opportunities by establishing connections with the mission of the university or college and the academic realm.

Opportunities. Campus ministries can be the catalyst for collaboration between faculty and student-affairs staff on planning a service-learning curriculum and social-justice programs and conferences. Many campus ministers have direct links to academic departments and can serve as service-learning educators. Many campus ministers possess a vast knowledge of human service needs and issues and a network of relationships with local community resources and human-service personnel, which can prove invaluable for educational endeavors. Campus ministers demonstrating their own commitment to community service can serve as important role models and mentors for students. As a wealth of post-college service opportunities abound for students to spend a year or more in domestic or international service, campus ministers can help graduating seniors explore these options. Campus ministers are well suited to facilitate students' movement to phase five (internalization) of the Service Learning Model, a lifelong commitment to service and social justice.

Cautions. Some service-learning programs within campus religious life have met with mixed success due to limited staffing resources or to attempts to do too much too quickly without a strong, viable student community; a comprehensive set of programs beginning with decisions on what kinds of programs and opportunities to create, including orientation for students, and eventually, provisions for reflection, require much time to develop. Many service programs and projects come from the student or campus community. With such grassroots support, these opportunities are generally more effective than others. Given the demanding nature and settings of some service experiences, campus ministers are encouraged to review their service placements for legal liability, especially those related to personal safety. Service experiences should also be reviewed from the standpoint of marketing. Since these experiences are sponsored by campus-ministry or religious-life organizations, students often feel they have to be religiously committed to participate; therefore, they miss valuable opportunities to discover or reflect on aspects of their faith. Providing a sense of freedom for and inclusion of all students can ensure a wider range of participants than those who are religiously affiliated. With the upsurge of volunteer and service-learning programs being developed on college campuses, the need for effective collaboration with established service programs also is vital. Often, student-affairs professionals have overlooked existing service-learning opportunities within campus ministries in their zeal to create a service-learning center, thus causing confusion, competition, and duplication of effort for the campus community. Effective structures of communication and collaboration are imperative to bring all involved with service together to discuss ideas and programs.

Conclusion

Essential to any vision of campus ministry is a faith in action directed toward service with disenfranchised individuals and communities. Enabling students to build bridges between their developing faith and their lived experiences through service, community, and reflection helps create world visions that allow for the renewal of human life. Campus religious life can have the finest worship, the most affirming fellowship groups, and the best retreat programs, but to what end, if this faith is not "other-directed" in service for and with justice? The development of faith is incomplete without experiences of service.

Service learning within the context of faith can provide viable avenues for student-affairs professionals to respond to and address students' spiritual needs. Campus ministers can assert their role as educators and provide links for collaboration between faculty, student-affairs professionals, and the broader community for the integration of service learning into the academic curriculum. Service is an area of ministry ripe for ecumenical collaboration between faith traditions.

Finally, service as a first step is not enough. Relationships formed through service, reflection within student communities, and faith enhanced through service experiences will propel students forward to create changes in their lives and world that will ensure social justice. These students will be the leaders in our faith and in our civic communities, bringing their insights about, sense of responsibility to, and solidarity with others into these settings.

References

Butler, J. (ed.). *Religion on Campus.* New Directions for Student Services, no. 46. San Francisco: Jossey-Bass, 1989.

Chamberlain, G. *Fostering Faith: A Minister's Guide to Faith Development.* New York: Paulist Press, 1988.

Fowler, J. *Faith Development and Pastoral Care.* Philadelphia: Fortress Press, 1987.

Healy, T.S.J. "Contemplatives in Action." *Georgetown University's Annual Report.* Washington, D.C.: Georgetown University Press, 1985.

McGinnis, J. *Educating for Peace and Justice: Religious Dimensions.* St. Louis, Mo.: Institute for Peace and Justice, 1984.

Parks, S. *The Critical Years: The Young Adult Search for a Faith to Live By.* San Francisco: Harper & Row, 1986.

Westerhoff, J. *Will Our Children Have Faith?* New York: Seabury Press, 1976.

Erin D. Swezey is the coordinator for community service at Loyola College of Maryland. Previously, she served as the director of campus ministry at Seattle University, Washington.

*The community can play a significant role in defining
students' values. Through combining rigor with relevance,
encountering new cultures, learning about power, and
discovering what it means to be a member of a society,
students can find their communities to be a powerful
source of their education.*

From Isolation to Commitment:
The Role of the Community in
Values Education

Steven K. Schultz

> We all, however, apprehend the land imperfectly, even when
> we go to the trouble to wander in it. Our perceptions are
> colored by preconception and desire . . . A man in
> Anaktuvuk Pass, in response to a question about what he did
> when he visited a new place, said to me, "I listen." That's
> all. I listen, he meant, to what the land is saying. I walk
> around it and strain my senses in appreciation of it for a
> long time before I, myself, ever speak a word. Entered in such
> a respectful manner, he believed, the land would open to him
> —Lopez (1986, p. 230)

Values are neither formed nor lived in a vacuum. They grow and take
their shape in a particular landscape—a landscape that must be understood if one is to act sensitively and effectively. As the above passage from
the book *Arctic Dreams* indicates, to gain a true sense of a landscape
requires from us a sense of appreciation, respect, and quiet listening. It
also requires an awareness of the preconceptions and desires that we
carry with us. The metaphor of exploring unknown terrain is suggestive
of the experience of those of our students who enter the community in
order to serve it, and, in a larger sense, of the relationship of the academy
itself to its neighboring communities.

The most effective values education we can provide for our students
is an intentional process of collaboration between academy and commu-

nity. To make such a statement is to challenge the way values education has been pursued previously and to raise questions of why and how a new approach might take place. Why should community service be integrated into the process of values education at all? What principles should guide our relationship to the communities in which we serve? If we have a "hidden moral curriculum," what does it teach our students?

As the Service Learning Model from Chapter One indicates, the process of moral development in students takes place gradually, moving from a stance characterized by a focus on the self, limited commitment, and inaction to a life-long concern for the larger world and its needs. The pages that follow will address the unique contribution that the community can make to the process of values development described by the Service Learning Model.

Four Aspects of the Community Role

There are four important areas where the community can make a contribution to the values education of secondary-school students. They are stated here in terms of student experience and include the following: *combining rigor with relevance, encountering new cultures and needs, learning the realities of power,* and *becoming a member of a group and of the larger society.* While each aspect is significant, the first is discussed at greater length, because of its pivotal importance to community service as a values-education methodology.

Combining Rigor with Relevance. In his books *The Reflective Practitioner* (1983) and *Educating the Reflective Practitioner* (1987), Donald A. Schön speaks of the dichotomy that has long existed in our educational process between *theory* and *practice, rigor* and *relevance.* Schön notes our common desire to avoid the uncertainties that characterize the world of practice by remaining at a level of abstraction. He calls for an educational process that is more context sensitive and explores some stimulating examples of what he calls "reflection-in-action." Schön's comments provide important insights for those involved in the process of teaching values.

There is perhaps no area where the connection between theory and practice is more important than the area of values education. Expressed values take on meaning only when they are realized in a tangible form in the life of a person. And yet, this problem of joining thought to action is the very one that Richard Morrill (1980) finds the least adequately addressed in his survey of recent practices of teaching values in college:

> Our earlier question concerning the relationship of knowledge to action, or of moral theory to practice, seems to fall decidedly short of receiving an adequate answer. Given that values, morality, and ethics

have to do precisely with deciding and choosing—with action—this particular relation between knowing and doing, by nature, presses for full connection. Yet, we find only partial answers, avoidance of the issue, or acceptance of the separation [p. 54].

In response to this surprising omission, service learning provides a model in which the effort to establish and maintain the connection between knowledge and action is central. Involvement in reflective community service offers students the opportunity to focus their concerns and set a more selfless, more other-directed agenda for the rest of their education.

Students who have participated in school-sponsored community-service programs regularly describe their service experience as a critical turning point in shaping the direction of their educational program as well as of their future vocational choice. In other words, the opportunity to encounter the needs of their community in a structured way has helped lend focus to the rigorous study they undertake in their academic program. We could say that this type of study is one that brings students out of themselves, from a morality that focuses upon logical consistency to one that allows students to act on their concerns.

What means are available to make certain that this link between rigor and relevance is maintained? It may be helpful here to think of the linking of rigor and relevance as depending on a two-way movement, from campus to community and from community to campus.

Moving from Campus to Community. Students can be encouraged to develop projects, both inside and outside the academic setting, that involve research on a community need and a focus on action. Commonly called action research, such projects allow students to see some tangible impact caused by their academic work.

Students in Westmont College's Urban Program work in small teams on "study-action" projects, combining library research with field study in the community through interviews on a topic of human need in a local city. In addition to developing a presentation for their fellow students, one of the results of their research is some form of action to address the need they have studied. During a recent semester, two students who studied the issue of hunger worked with Food Runners, a San Francisco group that encourages small-food businesses such as restaurants, catering services, and bakeries to deliver their surplus food to programs for the needy. The students were so inspired by the program that they began to explore the possibility of initiating a similar network in their home campus community.

Such research into community needs does not necessarily have to originate in an academic course. It can also originate in such program areas as those of a public-service center or a campus-ministries office. The research goal here may be to obtain input from the community about its most significant needs in order to develop new ideas for student projects. Faculty members can become quite enthusiastic about providing input into such a project if it makes direct use of their discipline and is done through student initiative.

In another approach, which begins with the campus and moves out to the community, faculty can become involved in linking rigor and relevance as respondents on a panel or as convocation speakers on topics of importance to the community. A series of lectures by faculty that apply their different disciplines to community needs can also be provocative and energizing for students. (Following the principle that the community is always the best source for a description of its own needs, the topic for such a series should be created through broad community input.)

Organizations that regularly use volunteers can be engaged in the process of service learning. Groups such as Habitat for Humanity, which make active use of individual and group volunteers to construct housing for the poor, can often provide both the chance for giving tangible service as well as for dialogue with community members about issues, such as why a housing shortage for the poor exists. Some organizations may be willing to organize an entire weekend retreat of service and study for a small group of students.

Some institutions, notably Thiel College in Pennsylvania, have taken service to the community as a central part of their mission. As a result of the difficult economic situation in the coal and steel industries of the surrounding region, the college decided to focus the research agenda of its various departments on ways to revitalize the local community. Faculty and students worked together to research the technical, economic, social, and psychological needs of the people of the local area and to explore how the expertise of the academy could meet those needs. It is clear that studying any discipline in such an atmosphere can powerfully shape how students understand the purpose of their learning. Wendell Berry (1987) has written that, recently, our approach to the goals of higher education seems to focus largely on the pursuit of personal gain, and yet "to make a commodity of it is to work its ruin" [p. 52]. Rather we need to understand that

> education in the true sense, of course, is an enablement to *serve*—both the living human community in its natural household or neighborhood and the precious cultural possessions that the living community inherits or should inherit. To educate is, literally, to "bring up," to bring young people to a responsible maturity, to help them to be good caretakers of what they have been given, to help them to be charitable toward fellow creatures [p. 52].

An institutionwide commitment like the one described above can have a powerful impact on the way students understand the purpose of their education. Jon Wagner (1988) provides a well-thought-out description of this vision of linking service with the research goals of the academic community.

Moving from Community to Campus. While community research by students and faculty represents one approach to bridging the gap between rigor and relevance, theory and practice, bringing community representatives to campus can be another means of accomplishing this goal. The size of activities of this type can range from very small to campus-wide, from informal meetings with small groups to large convocations, lectures, or all-day workshops.

A small-scale event may involve bringing a Salvadoran refugee to speak to students about her experiences before and after leaving her country. Inviting a staff member from a local group that serves the community of such refugees could give students tangible ideas about how they might respond to what they have learned. Including a faculty member from the Latin-American studies, political-science, economics, or religious-studies departments would help students understand the larger issues involved and why some actions may be more effective than others.

Large-scale efforts to link rigor and relevance include convocations and lectures to which a large number of students could be present. A panel of interested parties from the community who hold different opinions about an issue can spark debate and lead to action on the part of students. Such efforts should be connected to creative opportunities for student involvement following the presentation.

Summary. Whether they involve the commitment of one person or an entire institution, and whether they move from campus to community or bring community resources to the campus, several important principles must guide these efforts to link rigor and relevance:

• *Reflection* must be carefully built into every project to assure that students have sufficient background to understand an issue as well as why some actions may be more effective than others.

• *Opportunities for immediate action* should be one of the most carefully planned parts of the service-learning process. Students will need assistance in focusing the heightened awareness the research projects and lectures described above will produce in them. They also need service opportunities appropriate to their level of development. As the Service Learning Model presented in the opening chapter describes, students at different stages of growth can benefit from different kinds of experiences, which means that a range of prospects for action needs to be available to students to help them become involved in a way that will be most helpful to them.

• *Attention* must be paid to the process of personal development that each student is undergoing. If we are serious about seeing service learning as a means of values education, then we need to attend to the development of each student who participates. This can be done more directly through helping students examine their own relationship to the different phases described by the Service Learning Model, or more indirectly through the use of tools such as writing journals and performing group exercises.

Encountering New Cultures and Needs. One of the most significant benefits of many community-service experiences for students is the exposure such experiences give them to people different from themselves in race, class, culture, age, and life experience. What benefit does such exposure provide to values education? Charles Kammer (1988) writes that

> our experiences also shape our moral feelings and intuitions. Growing up in a white, middle-class neighborhood may make it very difficult for us to empathize with the pain, desolation, and difficulties of minorities or the poor in our culture. . . . Being immersed in a minority culture, becoming a minority in another culture, may help us to better understand and empathize with the situation of persons whom our society regularly degrades and dehumanizes. Such experiences may awaken new moral feelings in us and so offer us new moral possibilities [p. 29].

As part of their service-learning experience, students can be exposed to community events that speak to questions of racial and cultural differences. During a recent semester, students in the Westmont Urban Program attended a forum in the Latin community of San Francisco on images of Latin and Hispanic people in North American art and advertising. As the only nonminority people at the event, members of the group felt conspicuous. Toward the end of the evening, a student raised a question expressing his disbelief in the depiction of prejudice that the members of the panel had presented. The intense discussion that followed helped to deepen student understanding of the issue of race and the ways in which minority cultures are misunderstood and devalued by the majority culture. Students gained insight into the experience of others that they could not have gotten any other way.

Service learning can be the means for students to move from a sense of personal isolation to a sense of their place within a community. It can be a way to help students know more and care more about the places in which they live. By bringing them together with people who are different from themselves in culture, race, and economic status, it can help them see the common aspirations that all people share. From such learning, a new vision of community, one that is more inclusive and respectful of diversity, can begin to develop in our students.

The need for this changed vision is clear. A recent report by the National Conference of Mayors documented the growing physical, social, and economic isolation of the poorest sectors of our nation's cities. Like a living part of a body to which blood circulation has been cut off, these parts of our communities deteriorate in a spiral of poverty, crime, and drug abuse. The authors of *Habits of the Heart* (1985) speak of our nation dividing itself into "lifestyle enclaves": people joining exclusively with people like themselves in age, interests, race, economic status, and religious faith, as a replacement for the diversity of a real and vital community. On many of our nation's campuses, racial tensions and misunderstanding have grown in recent years, leading to incidents and outright violence.

What these indicators seem to show is that our country is becoming increasingly fractured across racial and economic lines. Traditional education in values misses the vital element that might help students actively address this fracturing—immediate contact with those who are different from themselves. It is remarkable to see the transformation that takes place in student attitudes and actions through the experience of knowing a Central American refugee or homeless individual as a person rather than as a symbol encountered through the media.

To be involved with people and situations first-hand is to take on people's life dilemmas as one's own. Wilfred Cantwell Smith provides a powerful description of the intent of this approach to education when he speaks of "critical corporate self consciousness" as what we should be striving for in our own development and that of our students (Smith, 1976): "critical," in that a sense of perspective always requires a certain distance—we must not become so identified with the group we are trying to serve that we loose our sense of perspective; "corporate," in that we acknowledge that any human social phenomenon cannot be understood entirely from the view of the outsider, but that we must acknowledge that we share to some extent the humanity of the person we study; "self conscious," in that in learning about others we also learn something of ourselves. Service learning provides the most vital opportunity to put this kind of attitude into practice.

Learning the Realities of Power. As the Service Learning Model indicates, the higher levels of moral development are characterized by an increasing concern for justice and for social transformation. Issues of socioeconomic power and control that may be invisible in the classroom become particularly important when it comes to planning strategy for community action. Ignorance in this area leads to ineffective action and disillusionment, and to a perpetuation of dependency among those who are in need.

Placing students in the service role without giving them the opportunity for reflection on the structural causes of needs creates the danger that their participation will help to preserve an unjust system. As John McKnight (1978) has pointed out, the service role can provide a sense of personal fulfillment to the server but disempower those who are served; therefore, an essential first part of the service-learning process needs to involve awakening students to issues of power.

If part of the meaning of justice includes participation in determining one's own destiny, then service learning that serves the ends of justice also requires the active involvement of the community in defining its own needs and how these will be met. Such sharing of power may present difficulties both administratively and academically, but without such sharing we give our students the message that the interests of those we serve do not really count. As mentioned in the introduction, it is through approaching with a sense of respect the unfamiliar landscape of the community that the community will open itself to us and we will begin to learn what it has to teach us.

Handled properly, a direct encounter with issues of power and justice can be an extremely productive learning experience for students. The Cornell University field program in New York City involves students in a group project each semester that marshals the talents of the students on behalf of the disenfranchised in that city. An issue chosen in advance by the instructor allows students to see how the power of vested interests affect those on the bottom of the social and economic ladder. On one occasion, students helped a community in extensive research that resulted in the preservation of a community market faced with the threat of demolition to make room for a real-estate development project.

Becoming a Member of a Group and of the Larger Society. A recently published book on moral philosophy (MacIntyre, 1984) suggests that an important part of the moral life of any society is handed down in what are called "practices," that is, cooperative activities within a society whose goods are internal to those activities. Actual practices can include such things as the nurturance of a family or society, the activities that constitute a profession like medicine, or even something as simple as the game of chess. From this perspective, the notion that one could "get ethics" from a single course in college or in a medical or business school is absurd. Rather we need to look carefully at the moral value already implicit in the *lived practices* of a society, beginning critically from this point rather than attempting to create the moral life *ex nihilo*.

Service learning allows students to participate in and observe the shared activities of our society in which our values are embedded. Service itself has its own inherent value, to be found in the activity itself and not in some end that it seeks. In this sense, service learning affords a valuable contrast to many of the activities in which we and our students participate, which tend to have an instrumental goal, whether grades or the next promotion, as their object. For example, at Georgetown University, fifty students each year are matched with developmentally disabled teen-agers. Through the "Best Buddies" program, students are given the oppor-tunity to share in a relationship based on friendship and common interests rather than intelligence and economic standing.

In addition, students involved in community service can become immersed in a large variety of practices that contain important values we share as a society. Whether he or she works in a free medical clinic in a refugee community, a neighborhood organization working for affordable housing, or an in-home care project for the elderly, the student is both learning and carrying on shared social values that extend beyond the limited private world. As Ernest Boyer (1987) has noted:

> The tradition of community, of placing one's life in a larger context is surely advanced as time is given to others. "In a lot of ways, college is an isolating experience," said a volunteer organizer. "These programs give students a sense that they live in the world, in a community" [p. 217].

The Service Learning Model speaks of the process of development from the phase of a student acting as an isolated individual to that of the student working in concert with others to achieve a goal. The "study action" projects described earlier are always done in groups, both to allow students to benefit from the results of others' work and to help them see that more can be accomplished by people working together.

Conclusion

Our pedagogy implies a worldview and a view of knowledge. What we might call the "hidden moral curriculum" of our institutions has placed undue emphasis on the individual and on moral reflection abstracted from a community context. As a result, students have difficulty connect-ing what they have learned in their course work with the very real needs of people they encounter beyond the confines of the campus.

Our communities and our world can no longer afford a moral edu-cation that encourages the isolation of reflection on values from lived reality. As a growing population competes for the planet's finite re-sources, unprecedented cooperation and involvement in community con-cerns will become even more important than they are now. Service in the community, combined with carefully designed study and reflection can begin to prepare students for the complex and often pain-filled world they will enter on graduation.

The Service Learning Model presented in the opening chapter of this volume demonstrates the importance of encouraging a reflective process in our students that will lead them from isolation and a limited commitment to the needs of others toward a broad concern for justice, lived out day by day, in the larger society. Service learning provides a way for students to bridge the separation between rigor and relevance and, in the process, to discover different needs and different cultures, to awaken to issues of power, and to learn what it means to be a member of a group. As this chapter has described, when encountered with respect, the community can play an essential role in this process of moral growth.

References

Bellah, R. N., Madsen, R., Sullivan, W. M., Swidler, A., and Tipton, S. M. *Habits of the Heart: Individualism and Commitment in American Life.* Berkeley: University of California Press, 1985.

Berry, W. *Home Economics.* San Francisco: North Point Press, 1987.

Boyer, E. *College: The Undergraduate Experience in America.* New York: Harper & Row, 1987.

Lopez, B. *Arctic Dreams: Imagination and Desire in a Northern Landscape.* New York: Bantam Books, 1986.

Kammer, C. L. *Ethics and Liberation.* Maryknoll, N.Y.: Orbis Books, 1988.

MacIntyre, A. *After Virtue: A Study in Moral Theory.* Notre Dame, Ind.: University of Notre Dame Press, 1984.

McKnight, J. "Professionalized Service and Disabling Help." In I. Illich (ed.), *Disabling Professions.* New York: Marion Boyars, 1978.

Morrill, R. L. *Teaching Values in College: Facilitating Development of Ethical, Moral, and Value Awareness in Students.* San Francisco: Jossey-Bass, 1980.

Schön, D. A. *The Reflective Practitioner.* New York: Basic Books, 1983.

Schön, D. A. *Educating the Reflective Practitioner: Toward a New Design for Teaching and Learning in the Professions.* San Francisco: Jossey-Bass, 1987.

Smith, W. C. *Religious Diversity.* San Francisco: Harper & Row, 1976.

Wagner, J. "Academic Excellence and Community Service: The Integrating Role of Undergraduate Internships." National Society for Internships and Experiential Education, Raleigh, N.C.: 1988.

Steven K. Schultz is the director of the Westmont College Urban Program in San Francisco. He has been involved in experiential education for the past ten years and is especially interested in the value of experience as a resource for ethical reflection.

The establishment of a working partnership between the
campus and community requires both partners to work
through a parallel process of assessment, program design,
implementation, and evaluation.

Joining Campus and Community Through Service Learning

Debbie Cotton, Timothy K. Stanton

Involving students in community-service learning requires campus program coordinators and community-agency staff to collaborate in program development. Often, because service-learning programs and community organizations have different goals and priorities, separate constituencies, and even varied organizational cultures, they design their programs independently and at cross-purposes. When this occurs, neither organization achieves its goals for students or for the community.

Successful service-learning programs bridge this gap between "town and gown" by cultivating a spirit of reciprocity, interdependence, and collaboration. When carefully considered, expressed, negotiated, and agreed upon, the needs and resources of each organization become complementary and mutually enhancing. This is not easy, however. Campus and community organizations may have competing goals, timetables, and agendas. Nevertheless, from the authors' experiences both on campuses and in communities following a program-design model and asking certain essential questions are the keys to establishing programs that effectively serve campus, community, and students.

Assessing and Determining Guidelines for the Partnership

As in launching any new partnership, campus and community organizations bring to service-learning relationships their particular sets of needs, expectations, and philosophies as to how the relationship should work.

However, because these are expressions of different communities with different experiences, they may conflict. The problems of both town and gown are real. Communication between the two communities is critical and each partner—the community agency and the campus program— must put forward and agree upon program goals and expectations. Many of these issues concern philosophical goals of the two parties. Establishing a philosophical base for community service is essential in procuring a collaborative relationship between the campus and the community. The following questions may be useful in determining this base:

What Responsibility Does an Institution Have to the Community? With the burgeoning popularity of student voluteerism, there is a great temptation on the part of campus staff to respond immediately to student initiatives and to place students in community service as quickly as possible. However, before placing students, staff, and if possible, student volunteers need to ask themselves the question: Is this service truly needed by the community? A more thoughtful (and ultimately more effective) process requires exploration of community problems in collaboration with community leaders, identifying along with them needs that students can effectively serve.

For example, before it designed and implemented a tutoring program, Stanford University's Haas Center for Public Service spent several months exploring with officials of a local school district various roles that students could play. The goal of the relationship, as viewed by both the Haas Center and the school district, is long-term school improvement for the district and experiential learning about the problems of urban schools for students.

What Responsibility Does the Campus Program Have to Students? Can eager but unprepared students do more harm than good? Without an understanding of what students are walking into, coordinators can inadvertently provide a service experience that has negative consequences for both students (discouraging them from community service forever) and agencies (where discouraged students fail to meet the needs of organizations). A frustrating experience with even one student can sour an agency on ever working with students "from that school" again. As a result, many campus programs practice preventive maintenance by offering prefield training and support. Cornell University's Field and International Study Program requires a preparation course for all students before they begin their service-learning experience (Giles, 1987; Whitham and Stanton, 1979).

What Responsibility Does the Community Have to the Campus Program? An influx of students into community agencies can be a mixed blessing. Students enter the community in September with big ideas, energy, and enthusiasm. By December, the attendance of these same students may become inconsistent because exams and papers demand more of their time. Due to this cyclical behavior, students may earn a reputation for being unreliable, and agencies become wary of greeting them with open arms.

Community organizations need to acknowledge the limitations of students' time and skills. With this understanding, they also need to think through how they will use students effectively and who in the agency will provide necessary training and supervision. If agencies have reservations about hosting student volunteers and if they have specific expectations of campus program staff, they should communicate these expectations to and negotiate them with campus staff before a program begins.

For example, the Field Studies Program at the University of California, Los Angeles, requires students to negotiate job responsibilities, expectations, and time commitments with the agency staff. The student and the agency supervisor sign a written contract that is also signed by the students' faculty sponsor and the Field Studies Office before the student begins his or her service experience.

What Responsibility Does the Community Have to Students? Taking on students requires a commitment by the agency. The students give their time in exchange for a work and learning experience. In return for their service, students want opportunities to talk with professional staff, to ask questions, and to learn how a community agency works to solve problems. Accepting this premise may require that an agency look critically at its human resources to determine how it will both use and support service learners. Student volunteers need both professional supervision and opportunities to learn about the broader issues in which an agency is involved. Organizations need to identify who will provide this and how it will be done.

For instance, the American Red Cross has a volunteer-development system. Potential volunteers are interviewed through the Volunteer Personnel Office, are made aware of the agency's priority needs, and work with a supervisor to structure a volunteer career path based on their interests. As a result of their investment in volunteer-management structures, the American Red Cross has a loyal core of long-term volunteers.

What Responsibility Does the Student Have to the Community? For many students, a service-learning experience may be their first exposure to working with people in need. It may be the first time that other people are significantly affected by their actions. Thus, student volunteers need to be reminded of basic job-skill manners such as contacting their agency if they are going to be late or if they will miss a day. Students may also need to be told about agency requirements for client confidentiality. While students can bring fresh ideas to the community, they need to be sensitive to the culture of the agency and have an understanding of appropriate strategies for initiating change. Campus programs need to identify how students will learn about the responsibilities and obligations of community service.

For the past seventeen years, students at The George Washington University in Washington, D.C., have participated through the School of Education in the Service Learning Course, with a required sixteen-hour-per-week internship. Not only are students briefed about the need for confidentiality, but they also examine their own prejudices about "people in need," reflect on their relationship to the community, and read and discuss contemporary fiction to develop their understanding of how a community works.

The five questions just discussed should be addressed by representatives of community organizations and campus service-learning programs as they contemplate working together. Having reviewed their responses and identified and assessed their ability to be strong partners in such a reciprocal and philosophically complementary relationship, they should be ready to work together.

Training and Supervision

Having decided to work together, and having determined the philosophical and practical nature of their relationship and the student service learning it will support, community organizations and campus programs may next turn their attention to issues of training and supervision. Typically, it is assumed that only the students need training before they go out to work in the community. However, there may also be a need to train faculty, campus staff, and agency personnel involved in the program.

The content and structure of training and supervision in service-learning programs will vary according to program goals and service tasks established. However, given that each constituency (faculty, campus staff, and agency personnel) has its own objectives for service learning (for example, faculty want students to learn more about specific issues, campus staff want students to grow personally, and agency staff need to get a job done), each constituency will need to be responsible for providing training and supervision that meets its particular objective for student volunteers. Again, a set of questions illuminating this "reciprocity principle" may be helpful.

What Training Resources Should Be Provided to Faculty or Program Staff Before They Send Students into the Community? Following the reciprocity principle, the campus program provides resources for the faculty on how to structure a service-learning experience that may be academically oriented, career-related, or faith-based. For example, at Brevard Community College in Florida, the faculty wanted service learning to be part of the curriculum, but they were not sure how to implement this idea. In order to incorporate service learning into the curriculum, the Service Learning Center staff developed a three-pronged approach that built in relevant training for faculty through the faculty-development program and organized a faculty advisory committee that persuaded key faculty and administrators to accept the values of and the need for service learning. In addition, the Service Learning Center staff devised a model course easily adapted to a variety of disciplines so that faculty did not have to reinvent a new service-learning curriculum for each course.

There are issues and skills involved in effectively placing students in community service with which campus staff should be familiar. As the Service Learning Model illustrates, it is important to assess a student's community-service background and to organize appropriate volunteer and reflection opportunities accordingly. For example, entering a student who has never been exposed directly to homeless people into a direct-service position at a homeless shelter may be overwhelming for the student and inappropriate. This may lead the student to drop out of the program and become soured on volunteerism altogether. It may be more appropriate to have this student initially serve in a one-day shelter clean-up project in a group setting. In this experience the student may not interact with the homeless, but he or she can become familiar with the environment of the homeless, learn about the homeless population, and receive recognition for his or her efforts. Campus staff must consider how they will assess the readiness of student volunteers and place them in appropriately challenging service experiences.

The Philadelphia Center of the Great Lakes Colleges Association has each student meet with a learning-process coordinator to discuss his or her interests and goals. Students complete an occupational assessment test, and the results are correlated with a computer database of community needs, developed from occupational assessment categories. The "high-tech, high-touch" approach is combined to give the best possible placement for the student volunteer.

What Training and Resources Should Be Provided to Agency Staff in Preparation for Working with Student Volunteers? When a community agency decides to bring student volunteers into their organization, they make an implicit commitment to hire a volunteer coordinator and train the staff to work effectively with volunteers. It is critical that a qualified staff person be designated as the volunteer coordinator and be given the time to administer the agency's volunteer program, acting as a bridge between staff and student volunteers. Agencies should conduct regular pre- and in-service training programs to enhance staff skills in effectively managing student volunteers.

The agency training program "Working with Student Volunteers," sponsored by the Volunteer Clearinghouse of Washington, D.C., used the

Service Learning Model as a tool to train agency personnel to assess students' developmental phases. This enabled agency staff to design appropriate student volunteer jobs.

What Training and Supervision Should the Campus Provide to Students? Here the reciprocity principle holds as well. The campus program provides training and supervision that relates to its objectives for student volunteers. Therefore, campus training might focus on making students self-managed volunteers and self-directed service learners, on helping them to learn from experiences and monitor and assess their service learning. As an example, the Community Involvement Center at San Francisco State University holds weekly small-group reflection meetings for their 146-member volunteer force. The reflection sessions are led by trained student volunteers and allow students to share and reflect on the successes and failures of their service-learning experiences.

What Training and Supervision Should the Agency Provide to Students? A well-designed agency training and supervision program will enable students to perform their jobs and grow personally at the same time. American Red Cross volunteers receive an annual briefing on the range of direct-service and leadership positions available, meet with their supervisor to review their performance, and then refine their volunteer-development plan. In this way, the Red Cross can move highly motivated people into leadership positions.

Other options for training students do exist. For instance, since school districts may be unable to, many campuses offer tutor-training seminars. In addition to task-oriented supervision, some community agencies offer students opportunities to reflect on their service experiences and provide them with an opportunity to learn about the organization's mission and challenges. It is suggested that campus programs and community organizations should agree on who is going to conduct training, supervision, and reflection that will meet each partner's objectives for a successful service-learning experience.

Assessment and Evaluation

Every partnership needs time for the parties to meet and assess their progress. In the case of service learning, there is also a need periodically to assess and evaluate whether the campus and community are continuing to derive expected benefits and are meeting their obligations to each other through their relationship.

In determining who is responsible for which aspect of this evaluation process, the reciprocity principle again applies. Each constituent is responsible for assessment and evaluation related to its objectives for the student's service-learning experience. It is important that the reciprocity principle be thoughtfully applied here because the objectives of each constituent are different and thus require different assessment and evaluation methods and criteria. We will again use a set of questions to discuss this issue.

What Responsibility Does the Campus Have to the Community? For the campus program, with its educational objectives, the fact that students successfully learn about and confront human problems may be a sufficient reward even if, in the eyes of the agency, the quality of the students' service is minimal. In the case of service learning for academic credit, campus faculty will be more interested in fact-based knowledge acquired as a result of the service experience rather than in the quality of the service provided. However, in attempting to develop a strong relationship between community and campus this one-sided approach will only lead to resentment by the agency of the campus' service program.

What Responsibility Does the Community Have to the Campus? Of course, the host-community organization will need to determine the actual contributions made by student volunteers in terms of service provided or problems solved. While they will understand the growth and development of volunteers as important, their assessment and evaluation will tend to focus more on the work accomplished, the need for which brought them into the service-learning relationship in the first place. Conversely, if the agency has a biased approach to assessment, this may lead to dissatisfaction on the part of the campus.

In similar fashion, the assessment process can be used by campus and community agency staff to evaluate their inter-program relationship over the long term. Is the campus observing anticipated benefits in its students? Are agency needs being met by student volunteers in a cost-effective way?

An example of this type of mutually beneficial relationship between the campus and community is a program where Georgetown University students staff the Calvary Shelter for homeless women at least three nights per week. Originally, Georgetown's intent was to allow students to work directly with homeless people, to have them develop a sense of responsibility, and to teach them how to cope with a variety of different situations. However, the experience of staffing the Shelter has touched students in a deeper way as they frequently give more hours than required, explore careers in social service and policy change, and sponsor educational programs on homeless issues on campus. In fact, many Georgetown alumni have gone on to staff the Shelter as professionals and serve on its board of directors.

If a service-learning program is perceived as a collaborative enterprise, then problems in the relationship will be mutually owned with both parties equally intent on finding solutions. Both parties need to take time to check with each other on a regular basis to monitor the partnership, and if needed, find ways to improve it. A mechanism for organizing this evaluation can be a faculty, student, and community advisory council, which might be charged with monitoring a service-learning program, providing a forum for expressing concerns, and developing new program models.

Establishing a Climate of Support

It is important to acknowledge that engaging in a partnership that supports student-service learning is probably not the first priority for either the campus or the community organization. Service learning for students is not the primary purpose of most educational institutions; nor is it the primary purpose of most human-service organizations. Unfortunately, the agency volunteer coordinators and the campus community-service staff are usually marginal to the main goals of their institutions and organizations. Thus, in order to function effectively with and on behalf of each other, they need to work together to support and affirm their relationship. To facilitate this, the following questions need to be addressed:

Why Build an Ethos for Service Learning? The campus programs that survive are those that build service learning into the mission and curricula of their institutions. If service learning is not clearly expressed as part of the institutional mission, it will not get sustained support from the faculty, trustees, community, or students. The program will get lost in the shuffle of extracurricular activities competing for students' time. Support on campus means that an ethos of service permeates the life of the school—from the mission statement to the spirit of community that grows from living out the mission. It will be expressed in public-relations materials and through adequate budgets for service programs.

Support off-campus means that student volunteers and those with whom they work are recognized and valued both inside the host-community organization and in the community at large. Community agency staff and their campus partners must work together to be sure that the off-campus community is aware of the contributions made by student volunteers. In turn, it is also important for the wider community to appreciate the work of community agencies in hosting and supervising student volunteers.

Why Is Recognition Important? Supportive partners deserve recognition. Part of the challenge of developing a climate of support for service learning depends on the ability of the community and campus to find ways to express recognition for their mutual accomplishments. By getting public recognition in the news media, obtaining student and agency recognition on campus, writing thank-you letters to an agency's board of directors, and other means, the collaborative relationship is supported, nurtured, and recognized.

Birmingham Southern College in Alabama has developed an on-going recognition program that goes beyond the usual annual awards banquet. Staff from community agencies audit college courses, faculty conduct "Lunch and Learn" seminars by lecturing on topics of interest at local community agencies, and the campus hosts an "executive in residence" who has freedom to research, lecture, and become rejuvenated from the daily grind of agency work. In this way, the campus maximizes its resources by recognizing agency contributions in a meaningful and mutually growth-enhancing way.

Conclusion

In addition to designing, implementing and evaluating a service rela-tionship between a campus program and a community organization, involved staff must be aware of the need constantly to build a climate of support from the community in addition to support from the campus for service learning. Without support from the educational institution and support from the agency and larger community, the partnership may not survive. Utilizing the Service Learning Model can be one of the first tools used by students, faculty, and agency staff to establish a common lan-guage and to develop an understanding of the special needs and strengths of college students in providing community service.

Quality service-learning programs do not just happen by sending students out to community agencies and hoping that they learn some-thing. A true partnership between the campus and the community takes time, people, and a commitment to develop the relationship and make it work. It is through such partnerships that the campus and community can truly join forces to create a collaborative and compassionate society.

References

Giles, D. E. "Getting Students Ready for the Field." *Experiential Education*, 1987, *11* (5), 1, 8.

Whitham, M., and Stanton, T. "Pre-Field Preparation: What, Why, How?" In S. E. Brooks and L. E. Althof (eds.), *Enriching the Liberal Arts Through Expe-riential Learning*. New Directions for Experiential Learning, no. 6. San Fran-cisco: Jossey-Bass, 1979.

Debbie Cotton is former director of Youth Services of the Volunteer Clearinghouse of the District of Columbia. Currently, she is exploring new dimensions in the relationship between campus and community in her graduate studies at Boston College.

Timothy K. Stanton is associate director of the Haas Center for Public Service at Stanford University. He has been involved in service learning for the past eighteen years, serving on both sides of the campus-community fence.

*Through university and college case studies, the Service
Learning Model is illustrated by outlining characteristics of
each phase, as well as by discussing problems and potential
for change inherent in each institution's circumstances.*

Transforming the University Through Service Learning

Sharon G. Rubin

How do we think about colleges and universities? We describe them as
ivory towers; we sing about ivy-covered walls. Whether a campus has
arched entrances with wrought-iron gates or merely a major U.S. highway
to provide a boundary, most of us take pleasure in seeing our campuses
as havens, set apart from society's problems, and offering time and space
for contemplation and scholarship. The college that springs to mind as
our ideal may have red brick buildings with white pillars or Gothic
stained glass, but it is a restricted community of teachers and learners,
not an open community responsive to social problems.

Of course, many of us would argue that despite their separateness,
our campuses are indeed involved in the life of the larger community.
After all, the mission statement of almost every college in the country
advocates the ideal of good citizenship for students, to say nothing of
concern for others. Consequently, students perform internships, participate in cooperative education, and are involved in service projects. Government and foundation grants, institutes, and think tanks give faculty a
chance to use their expertise to grapple with important social problems.
Local residents who attend campus events are welcomed. However, the
tension between the campus as a protected environment and the campus
as an active participant in the "real world" is unlikely to disappear. The
issue then becomes not whether the campus and the community can be
related so inextricably that the boundary between them dissolves, but
where that boundary should be.

In thinking about how to determine where that boundary is on our
own campuses, and to judge where that boundary belongs, the same sort

of developmental framework that helps us understand student growth and capacity for change can help us understand our institutions as well. The developmental phases used earlier in this volume in the Service Learning Model—exploration, clarification, realization, activation, and internalization—can also be used to describe the phase a campus as a whole is in and how a transition between phases can be promoted.

Developmental Phases: Case Studies

It is perhaps easier to identify how an individual can be helped or hindered in the developmental process than how an institution can be. However, the same notion of correct balance of challenge and support that underlies many developmental theories can also be used to analyze institutions. What in the campus environment supports the present strengths of the college, and what challenges the college to live up to new potential? What roles do administrators, faculty, students, and community organizations play in supporting a particular phase of service-learning development or in challenging the college to go on to the next stage? What are some symptoms that an institution is "stuck" at a particular developmental level, and what might provide the new perspectives or actions that promote growth?

Following are several hypothetical cases based on many different examples from actual colleges. They illustrate some characteristics of each phase, as well as problems and the potential for change inherent in each college's circumstances.

Exploration. Ordway State College, a medium-sized campus with a longstanding reputation for small classes and a caring faculty, is typical of colleges just beginning to think about community service. A few faculty on campus, in psychology and social work, have always had their students spend some hours over the course of a semester in a nursing home or day-care center. A few sororities and fraternities put on dances to raise money for charities or collect canned goods at holiday time. The college president has attended a Campus Compact presentation at an educational conference and come away with a vague feeling that Ordway should be doing more to promote good relationships between the college and the community. The dean of students is attempting to do just that with a town-gown coalition. Although there are examples on campus of provisions for good community service, nobody speaks for the entire college and nobody coordinates activities.

Suddenly, a few fortunate circumstances occur. The new academic dean has come from a school more heavily involved in service and mentions this to a sociologist who has just come back inspired by a presentation she heard at a workshop. Before the week has passed, they have gathered an informal group of a few student leaders, some faculty, and an interested administrator or two, and they begin to discuss service plans for the curriculum, for student activities, even for a network of community organizations.

Does a transition to the next stage now occur? Not automatically. Fortunately, Ordway does not make the mistake of many other colleges, which get so bogged down trying to "reinvent the wheel" that they end up with a square one. Group members need to begin by asking the right questions. What is happening on campus? Has anyone ever done a survey of all campus groups or faculty to determine their level of community activity? Are such terms as "internships," "cooperative education," "public service," "field work," and "action research" included so that those using different terms recognize their activities? Has anyone collected articles on what similar colleges have been able to create? Has everyone called friends at other colleges to find out if they can recommend any program models worth further investigating? Has anyone talked informally with the school's president, or with other academic and student-affairs administrators, to find out whether or not potential support can be found? Has anyone investigated the resources national organizations can provide: written materials, consultants, program examples, a peer network?

If the informal Ordway group collects good information, remains open to new members and new ideas, and does not get discouraged by how much longer everything takes than planned, the clarification phase is usually the result.

Clarification. Solon College is a liberal arts college with a reputation for nurturing students. Whatever students suggest is taken very seriously. Currently students seem interested in community service, so activities connected with service are cropping up all around campus. A philosophy professor is rethinking a course on social justice to respond to a student desire for active involvement in the solution of social problems. The "Greek" adviser encourages sorority members who are thinking about sponsoring a community-service project rather than merely holding fund-raising dances. The academic dean proposes a speakers' series so that thoughtfulness about service accompanies campus activism. Local volunteer coordinators, delighted by the informal news emanating from the campus, make more and more requests for student help.

However, as the projects increase, program directors' tempers flare. Programs with the same goals but called by different names find themselves on the defensive. Departmental internship courses, a long-standing cooperative education program, even a cooperative project of the service fraternity, the campus ministries, and several community organizations are suddenly competing with a number of different kinds of new community-service projects. A few people begin to say, "There's too much going on, and we can't be sure of the quality of what everyone is doing."

At budget time, there is a set of competing requests. At first, administrators try to get representatives of different program types to come together to decide on priorities, but after several unsuccessful attempts, a token amount is given to each group. Everyone is overworked and underfunded.

If a campus gets stuck in the clarification phase, there will still be some major successes, due to student enthusiasm. However, some programs will not survive the Darwinian environment, and student disappointment and cynicism over territoriality may eventually undercut even seemingly strong programs.

Is Solon making a mistake by being too responsive to students? In at least one sense, it is. By trying to do everything at once, it doesn't have time to learn from experience. Several pilot projects of different kinds, carefully planned and evaluated, as well as a thorough evaluation of existing programs, will give Solon a sense of what is both feasible and desirable. It may even be necessary to wait for a period of time before an informed decision can be made about directing major funding to a limited number of programs or projects, a difficult thing for a college that prides itself on quick responsiveness. It is only through completing a process of clarification, however, that the next phase can begin.

Realization. Greenstone University prides itself on the commitment it has made to community service. Its president has been speaking forcefully and persuasively not only to the campus and the larger academic community but also to the board of trustees about the necessity to involve students in service. The trustees have responded with a pledge to make scholarship funds available to assure that every student, no matter what his or her financial status, can participate. There are a number of strong student-run projects, and most students engage in some form of service.

There is so much satisfaction on the part of students, faculty, and administrators alike about what students are able to accomplish that Greenstone believes it could not improve upon its ideas. As a university with strong support from top-level administrators, excellent funding, and intense student involvement, it has reason to be proud, but realization is not the last stage of development. Greenstone's programs are not integrated into the curriculum. Although faculty are happy to have students participate in life off-campus, they have not rethought their own major requirements in terms of community service, the ways in which service can be pertinent to their disciplines, or the interdisciplinary potential of such service. Because community service stands outside the ongoing intellectual life of the university, it is not permanent to campus life, as the president and the campus believe. If the president retires, if the political climate changes, if student interest wanes, a program that is a national model today may disappear tomorrow. For instance, University Year for Action programs, a kind of federally funded domestic Peace Corps, were extremely popular in the early 1970s. Welcomed by campuses and their surrounding communities, they gave many undergraduates an opportunity for twelve months of full-time service. However, with little faculty involvement in supervision and evaluation, with varied schemes for academic credit unrelated to general education or requirements for majors, with dependence on a small group of enthusiastic proponents, and with reliance on external funding, most of these programs were never truly institutionalized and so sank without a trace at many universities within a few years.

Activation. Midwest River University has programs less elaborate than Greenstone's, but it has a set of community-service activities that are the thoughtful result of sustained interest and commitment. Administrators such as the dean of students have worked systematically over the years to coordinate service programs for the university, to maintain the size and quality of the programs, and to take an active role in collaborating with faculty interested in integrating community-service projects into their courses. The campus curriculum committee completed a review of general educational requirements several years ago and recommended that at least one general education course in each department include a voluntary community-service component. As one member of the curriculum committee noted, "James O. Freedman, the president of Dartmouth College, helped us understand that education must include not only an examination of thought but an examination of action. In an interview in the *New York Times,* Freedman stated that the goal of a college education is to help students develop a public self and a private self, the self that can be alone at three o'clock in the morning, and to find a way to have those selves converse with each other and form a whole human being (1987). The public self is the self that must act in society. If we don't give students an intellectual and moral framework and a chance to test it out, we're not fulfilling the purpose of general education." Spurred on by the curriculum committee's reexamination of general education, many departments have rethought the content of their major requirements, and several have created senior capstone courses that combine conceptualization with application in the community.

Faculty enthusiasm is tempered by practical concern. Many faculty have not had the experience of placing students in community programs, and they want to make sure that the same high standards they expect in the classroom are maintained in a new environment. However, their commitment to a form of education that does not separate knowledge from behavior, understanding from experience (Palmer, 1987), is so powerful that faculty are finding authorities to help them become their own experts. "We do this in every field—we build on the intellectual work of others. This will just be a whole new sphere of expertise for most of us," adds one faculty member who was initially a skeptic. What changed his mind? "I am seeing the results in my students' ability to ask the important questions, so they're pulling me along with them!"

Little by little, the educational goals at Midwest River are being rethought and reshaped to integrate service and learning. All members of the university see themselves as responsible for this mission, and a seamless curriculum is emerging as a result.

Internalization. Beneficence College is a small, rural liberal arts college that is affiliated with a religious denomination. A number of years ago, it went through the same sort of process, on a miniature scale, that Midwest River University is now undergoing. The result was similar in some ways to what is occurring at Midwest River, but in others it was very different. Because the college is in a rural area, there are not many opportunities for students to be involved in ongoing community service. It is not that the needs do not exist, but there is very little organized response to those needs. However, the lives of Beneficence and the community are intimately intertwined, nonetheless.

Because the process by which Beneficence reached internalization involved reconceptualizing its educational goals, Beneficence changed its mission statement. That statement now asks students and faculty to commit themselves to lives of moral action through the educational process. The entire campus has become a think (and do) tank for the surrounding community. Individuals, groups, and government agencies are encouraged to work with the faculty and students at Beneficence to address their needs. A campus coordinator of community service evaluates each request and then takes it to the appropriate faculty member or members, who share it with their students. In collaboration with those requesting help, projects are undertaken in the context of a course, department, or campus organization. If the issue is complex, a town meeting is called, and resources are sought from the entire campus community to work toward a response. The college has never let the community, or itself, down.

Students at Beneficence admit that they are frequently overwhelmed initially but are proud of their ability as educated people to marshal their knowledge, skills, and commitment to undertake whatever comes their way. They have come to believe that the combination of research and action is particularly powerful. They have also learned that from their diverse talents, and those of the community, new and creative problem-solving capabilities frequently and unexpectedly change.

The faculty were initially concerned that the rigor they demand from students working on solutions to real problems, combined with the experimental nature of the curriculum, would result in a decline in the number of students interested in Beneficence, but applications have tripled over the past three years. "We didn't know what to expect," the president noted, "but I think we are meeting some very deep need in young people. Over and over, they tell me, 'I want to make a difference; I want to do it with people who share my values and my idealism. That doesn't mean that I don't want to be what the world calls successful. But this college will give me the chance to make a difference.' Every time I wake up at night filled with anxiety about the transformation of our college, I hear those voices and I know we have made the right decision."

Greenstone is not Ordway or Solon; Midwest River is not Benefi-cence. Every college puts the boundary between the campus and the community at a different place when it defines its educational and service missions. Although some colleges do change their natures radically, most will make incremental changes within phases or between them. Each phase, each stage, brings with it the questions:

- How do we know we are doing a good job?
- What are the responsibilities of students, faculty, administrators, community organizations, and those served?
- What are our responsibilities to each participant in the service process?
- Are there educational principles that transcend the particular details of our programs?
- Are there ways to measure the solidity of our accomplishments?

Principles of Good Practice That Combine Service and Learning

At a recent Wingspread conference, sponsored by the Johnson Foundation and a number of national organizations, including the National Society for Internships and Experiential Education, the American Association for Higher Education, Campus Compact, the Council of Chief State School Officers, the National Association of Independent Schools, the National Association of Secondary School Principals, Youth Service America, and the Constitutional Rights Foundation, representatives of many different types of schools, colleges, programs, and organizations came together to answer these questions by refining the principles of good practice that combine service and learning. Ten principles withstood the scrutiny of the group. Together, they embody the broadest agreement on standards. They can be used by a psychology professor who takes students to a nursing home or as principles for major curricular reform, by a fraternity running a used clothing drive or to organize a campus-community literacy project. Following are the principles and a brief amplification of each, with the permission of the Johnson Foundation (1989).

1. *An effective service-learning program engages people in responsible and challenging actions for the common good.* Participants in programs combining service and learning should engage in tasks that they and society recognize as important. These actions should require reaching beyond one's range of previous knowledge or experience. Active partici-

pation—not merely being a spectator or visitor—requires accountability for one's actions, involves the right to take risks, and gives participants the opportunity to experience the consequences of those actions for others and for themselves.

2. *An effective service-learning program provides structured opportunities for people to reflect critically on their service experience.* The service experience alone does not ensure that either significant learning or effective service will occur. It is important that programs organize opportunities for participants to think about their experiences and what they have learned. Through discussions with others and individual reflection on moral questions and relevant issues, participants can develop a better sense of social responsibility, advocacy, and active citizenship. This reflective component allows for personal growth and is most useful when it is intentional, continuous throughout the service experience, and provides the opportunity for feedback. Ideally, feedback will come from those persons being served, as well as from peers and program leaders.

3. *An effective service-learning program articulates clear service and learning goals for everyone involved.* From the outset of the project, service participants and recipients alike must have a clear sense of the goals both of what is to be accomplished and what is to be learned. These goals must be arrived at through negotiations with all parties and in the context of the traditions and cultures of the local community. Service-learning goals should reflect the creative and imaginative input of those providing the service as well as those receiving it. Attention to this important factor of mutuality in the service-learning exchange protects against the "service" becoming patronizing charity.

4. *An effective service-learning program allows for those with needs to define those needs.* The actual recipients of service, as well as the community groups and constituencies to which they belong, must have the primary role in defining their own service needs. Community-service programs, government agencies, and private organizations can be helpful in defining what service tasks are needed and when and how these tasks should be performed. This collaboration to define needs will ensure that service by participants will not take jobs from the local community and will involve tasks that will otherwise go undone.

5. *An effective service-learning program clarifies the responsibilities of each person and organization involved.* Several parties are potentially involved in any service and learning program: participants (students and teachers, volunteers of all ages), community leaders, service supervisors, and sponsoring organizations, as well as those individuals and groups receiving the services. It is important to clarify the balance of roles and responsibilities of these parties through negotiation as the program is

being developed. Such negotiation should include identifying and assigning responsibility for tasks to be done, while acknowledging the values and principles important to all the parties involved.

6. *An effective service-learning program matches service providers and service needs through a process that recognizes changing circumstances.* Because people are often changed by the service-learning experience, effective programs must build opportunities for continuous feedback about the changing service needs and growing service skills of those involved. Ideally, participation in the service partnership affects personal development in areas such as intellect, ethics, cross-cultural understanding, empathy, leadership, and citizenship. In effective service-learning programs, the relationships between groups and individuals are dynamic and often create dilemmas. Such dilemmas may lead to unintended outcomes. They can require recognizing and dealing with various individuals and groups of people.

7. *An effective service-learning program expects genuine, active, and sustained organizational commitment.* In order for a program to be effective, it must have a strong, ongoing commitment from both the sponsoring and the receiving organizations. Ideally, this commitment will take many forms, including reference to service learning in the organizational mission statement. Effective programs must receive administrative support, become line items in the organization's budget, be allocated appropriate physical space, equipment, and transportation, and allow for scheduled release time for participants and program leaders. In schools, the most effective service-learning programs are linked to the curriculum and require that the faculty become committed to combining service and learning as an integral part of their teaching.

8. *An effective service-learning program includes training, supervision, monitoring, support, recognition, and evaluation to meet service-learning goals.* The most effective service-learning programs are sensitive to the importance of training, supervision, and monitoring of progress throughout the program. This is a reciprocal responsibility and requires open communication between those offering and those receiving the service. In partnership, sponsoring and receiving organizations should recognize the value of service through appropriate celebrations, awards, and public acknowledgement of individual and group service. Planned, formalized, and ongoing evaluation of service-learning projects should be part of every program and should involve all participants.

9. *An effective service-learning program ensures that the time commitment for service learning is flexible, appropriate, and in the best interests of all involved.* In order to be useful to all parties involved, some service activities require longer participation or a greater time commitment than others. The length of the experience and the amount of time required are

determined by the service tasks involved and should be negotiated by all the parties. Sometimes a program can do more harm than good if a project is abandoned after too short a time or given too little attention. Where appropriate, a carefully planned succession or combination of participants can provide the continuity of service needed.

10. *An effective service-learning program is committed to program participation by and with diverse populations.* A good service-learning program promotes access and removes disincentives and barriers to participation. Those responsible for participation in a program should make every effort to include and make welcome persons from differing ethnic, racial, and religious backgrounds, as well as varied ages, gender, economic levels, and those with disabilities. Less obvious, but very important, is the need for a sensitivity to other disincentives, such as lack of transportation, family, work and school responsibilities, concern for personal safety, or uncertainty some may have about their ability to make a contribution.

Where Do We Go from Here?

The combination of progressive developmental phases as outlined in the Service Learning Model and the standards advanced at the Wingspread conference provide powerful tools by which to measure both individual and institutional progress. Research on the model and the standards in the context of different types of colleges, programs, and students, will allow us to address some important questions about our educational convictions and practices:

• Do we believe a goal of higher education is to make education personally meaningful for each student? What opportunities do we provide for students to create meaning from their college experiences? How does service learning affect the ability of students to create meaning?

• Do we believe that students should develop a life philosophy that includes social responsibility? Do we provide opportunities for students to act as socially responsible citizens? How does service learning affect the ability of students to adopt meaningful social philosophies?

• Do we believe that the resources of a college—faculty, students, knowledge, budget—should be used to serve the community? What is the extent and type of relationship we should have with the community? Should the boundary between campus and community be shifted? How does service learning affect the location of that boundary?

• Do we believe that service learning should be carried out with the highest possible standards? What administrative or program structures do we need in order to offer service learning that meets our educational goals and standards?

The answers to these questions may lead to even broader and deeper inquiries about the role of higher education in society. At the very least, however, they will lead to a vision of an institution transformed through service learning and a plan for its accomplishment.

Annotated Bibliography

Bellah, R. N., Madsen, R., Sullivan, W. M., Swidler, A., and Tipton, S. M. *Habits of the Heart: Individualism and Commitment in American Life.* New York: Harper & Row, 1985.

This volume, on the conflict between personal individualism and Americans' need for community and commitment to one another, sets out the philosophical themes that underlie practical issues in service learning.

Boyer, E. L. *College: The Undergraduate Experience in Higher Education.* New York: Harper & Row, 1987.

This assessment of higher education, based on extensive research on thirty public and private colleges, offers a number of recommendations relating to student service in the community. The entire volume is useful in providing background and context for the issue of how higher education can promote service learning.

Brooks, S., and Altho, J. (eds.). *Enriching the Liberal Arts Through Experiential Learning.* New Directions for Experiential Education, no. 6. San Francisco: Jossey-Bass, 1979.

A number of perspectives on the relationship of various forms of experiential learning to liberal-arts goals are presented. Chapters on prefield preparation for experience and a philosophical rationale for experiential learning in the liberal arts are particularly relevant for service-learning program development.

Chickering, A. (ed.). *The Modern American College: Responding to the New Realities of Diverse Students and a Changing Society.* San Francisco: Jossey-Bass, 1981.

This massive volume covers a full range of challenges that colleges and universities face in the light of changing demographics and social goals. Chapters on moral development, experiential learning, and program models for service are particularly germane.

Greenleaf, R. K. *Teacher as Servant: A Parable.* New York: Paulist Press, 1979.

This fictional account of a freshman who joins a seventy-student "house" on his college campus to engage in service to others is not unrealistic, merely unrealized in current higher education.

Kendall, J. (ed.). *Combining Service Learning: A Resource Book for Community and Public Service*. Raleigh, N.C.: National Society for Internships and Experiential Education, 1989.

This volume is the most complete compilation of writings on service learning available. Many of the selections are no longer obtainable through other sources.

Kendall, J., Duley, J. S., Little, T. C., Permaul, J. S., and Rubin, S. *Strengthening Experiential Education Within Your Institution*. Raleigh, N.C.: National Society for Internships and Experiential Education, 1986.

A manual for faculty and administrators interested in developing or strengthening service and other experiential programs, this volume takes up such issues as building experiential learning into the mission and values of a college, integrating service learning into the curriculum, increasing faculty involvement, ensuring quality, and establishing appropriate administrative structures.

Kolb, D. A. *Experiential Learning: Experience as the Source of Learning and Development*. Englewood Cliffs, N.J.: Prentice-Hall, 1984.

Kolb's theoretical model of experiential learning is widely used by the service-learning community in designing experience-based programs; it provides a justification for combining reflection and conceptualization with service.

Little, T. C. (ed.). *Making Sponsored Experiential Learning Standard Practice*. New Directions for Experiential Learning, no. 20. San Francisco: Jossey-Bass, 1983.

Although this volume deals with the general issue of how experiential learning can become an ongoing part of the mission of a university, those interested in service learning should find the strategies discussed helpful as well.

Luce, J. (ed.). *Service Learning: An Annotated Bibliography*. Raleigh, N.C.: National Society for Internships and Experiential Education, 1988.

This thoughtful and complete bibliography covers such topics as definitions and the history of service, the theoretical and philosophical roots of service, service learning in higher and secondary education, implications for practice, research, and resources.

Wagner, J. "Teaching and Research as Student Responsibilities: Integrating Community and Academic Work." *Change*, 1987, *19* (5), 26–35.

Wagner dismisses the dichotomy between community service and academic learning, arguing convincingly that each enhances the other and that the combination of the two has a number of specific benefits for students, faculty, and universities.

Resource Organizations

Campus Compact: Project for Public and Community Service, Box 1975, Brown University, Providence, R.I. 02912 (401–863–1119).

Campus Compact, an organization of over two hundred college and university presidents, attempts to influence public policy on community service and inspire program development and expansion of member campuses.

Campus Outreach Opportunity League (COOL), 386 McNeal Hall, University of Minnesota, St. Paul, Minn. 55108 (612–624–3108).

COOL, a student-organized and student-led group, sponsors regional workshops and an annual conference, offers a newsletter and consulting services, and advocates student participation in program development and implementation.

National Society for Internships and Experiential Education (NSIEE), 3509 Haworth Drive, Suite 207, Raleigh, N.C. 27609 (919–787–3263).

NSIEE is an educational organization of over a thousand individual members and several hundred colleges and universities. It provides resources such as a national conference, a bimonthly newsletter, individualized reference searches, and consulting services for the higher-education and secondary-education communities. It also publishes a wide range of materials such as bibliographies, national directories, occasional papers, and program manuals.

National Youth Leadership Council, 1910 West County Road B, Roseville, Minn. 55113 (612–631–3672).

The NYLC is a nonprofit organization dedicated to developing service-oriented youth leaders. It publishes a newsletter, offers a teachers' institute on service learning, and sponsors workshops and conferences.

Youth Service America, 1319 F Street, N.W., Suite 900, Washington, D.C. 20004 (202–783–8855).

An advocate for public policy supporting conservation corps and community-service programs in colleges, high schools, and middle schools, YSA publishes a newsletter and position papers.

References

Johnson Foundation. "Principles of Good Practice in Combining Service and Learning." Wingspread Conference, Racine, Wis., 1989.

Palmer, P. "Community, Conflict, and Ways of Knowing." *Change,* 1987, *19* (5), 20–25.

"Redefining Dartmouth: New President's Quest for 'Private Selves.' " *New York Times,* August 23, 1987.

Sharon G. Rubin is dean of the Charles R. and Martha N. Fulton School of Liberal Arts, Salisbury State University, Salisbury, Maryland, and president of the National Society for Internships and Experiential Education.

Index

Ordering Information

New Directions for Student Services is a series of paperback books that offers guidelines and programs for aiding students in their total development—emotional, social, and physical, as well as intellectual. Books in the series are published quarterly in Fall, Winter, Spring, and Summer and are available for purchase by subscription as well as by single copy.

Subscriptions for 1990 cost $42.00 for individuals (a savings of 20 percent over single-copy prices) and $56.00 for institutions, agencies, and libraries. Please do not send institutional checks for personal subscriptions. Standing orders are accepted.

Single copies cost $12.95 when payment accompanies order. (California, New Jersey, New York, and Washington, D.C., residents please include appropriate sales tax.) Billed orders will be charged postage and handling.

Discounts for quantity orders are available. Please write to the address below for information.

All orders must include either the name of an individual or an official purchase order number. Please submit your order as follows:
   Subscriptions: specify series and year subscription is to begin
   Single copies: include individual title code (such as SS1)

Mail all orders to:
Jossey-Bass Inc., Publishers
350 Sansome Street
San Francisco, California 94104